Under the Red Tin Roof
A Memoir

Josephine Zamora Padilla

DEDICATION

To my ancestors who provided me with the
motivation and inspiration
to carry on the tradition of storytelling.

CONTENTS

ACKNOWLEDGMENTS

Some of the information is pulled from recorded dialog, many from memory, some from census materials. There are no composed characters. The chronology of certain events has been altered in an effort to make a clear point. Seen through the eyes of a child and adult who has experienced these lives. Everything is as accurate as I recall.

I have interviewed my siblings, Candie Herrera, Cecilia Bachicha, and Frances Padilla. My late niece Carmen Lou Padilla and I interviewed and audio taped my Father Santiago over 20 years ago therefore I feel it important to acknowledge her as well. My first cousins Bessie Torres and Virginia Romero also recalled events as did a childhood friend Orlando Lopez. In addition, I translated some information from sections of "Al Pie de La Sierra" by Javier E. Sanchez. His book is extremely detailed 1829 – 1950 and I highly recommend it. Some facts about Torrance County I found on the county website.

My husband J.M. (Jose) Padilla has provided invaluable assistance by having me rewrite sections in order to make a clear point and has proof read my manuscript.

I was unable to locate relatives of Don Ponceano Sanchez while visiting Abo, N.M. His poem has been near and dear to my heart since I was a child and I was able to identify his home.

A very special Thank You to Larry Allen who is proficient with software and he was instrumental and an enormous asset in bringing this book to publication.

PREFACE

I started researching and documenting the lives of my ancestors in 2017 when my Husband J.M. (Jose Manuel) was away walking the 525 mile stretch of the Camino de Santiago de Campostela from France to Spain. It had been placed on the back burner and now this pandemic of Covid 19 has afforded me time to return to my project as our state has strict stay at home and social distancing restrictions. We have had to put numerous events and commitments on hold.

During a time when many people are finding themselves bored, lonely, or moderately depressed I have been rewarded as I delve into my past and reminisce about nostalgic scenes from my childhood. This project has forced me to explore the depths of my upbringing while revealing the timeless spirit of the land as I have ventured out to revisit many places. It has given me an intuitive understanding as to my roots. I more clearly understand that one can live under the same roof with the same set of parents and environment and yet come to a totally different perception of the events that took place which in turn have a lasting effect on our lives and the decisions we therefore make.

My ancestor stories invited me to reflect on my own life and I feel they can touch on other people's stories and memories. They have challenged me to use my imagination, look at the truth, inspire questions, and had me look for answers which at times have gotten under my skin

We have the choice to dwell on being victims of our past or to grow, evolve and overcome hang-ups and self-imposed limitations and choose instead to love ourselves.

I have wondered how our ancestors must have felt when they endured the influenza in the 1918-1919 when it spread worldwide. It is estimated that about 500 million people or one-third of the world's population became infected with this virus. Certainly, they did not have the technology to connect via Zoom meeting, e-mails, texting, Aura frames or phones.

1 INTRODUCTION

"UNDER THE RED TIN ROOF" 7 children suddenly became maternal orphans in 1952. Our ages ranged from 3 to 21. This memoir is about those broken hearts and broken lives. Our Mother's death impacted each family member differently. Mother's death had a profound effect on our Father as well.

At inception my goal was to provide a "Zamora" family genealogy. In so doing I was enveloped in the individual and very colorful, interesting lives they each lived. I observed and came to realize the importance that these ancestors played in my personal story. I feel that we are molded by those people and in addition one's surroundings growing up also had an impact. I was proud to live under "The Red Tin Roof" and knew that it is a very recognized landmark in Torrance County.

Why did my Grandfather Eleno return to his ancestral home? What pulled at his heart strings? According to my father's understanding his "Papa Eleno" fled Manzano in 1860 and relocated to Santa Fe at the age of 15 to escape his abusive Stepfather Mr. Archuleta. Was it really the abuse? Was he still mourning his Father Jose de Jesus Blas's sudden death at a brawl in a bar two years earlier or was he simply a rebellious teenager? Now living in Santa Fe, he lied about his age in order to enlist in the military. He served during the Civil War, was twice wounded, received an honorable discharge in 1866, and returned to Santa Fe "The Land of Enchantment" where he married Anastacia Chavez.

At 37 he returned to Manzano a widower with 4 children to raise. Eventually he remarried Grandmother Vicenta and the family grew to 13 now living under "The Red Tin Roof". That roof holds countless stories spanning several

Zamora generations including: a successful mercantile business for over 40 years, has survived a fire, a flood, births, deaths, weddings, dances, heartbreaks, a community hub, and so much more.

Embedded in this memoir is our culture, struggles with adverse weather, the presence of Apache and Navajo Indians that Juan Jose Archuleta encountered in route to Missouri, wildlife, crops, music, poems, religion, national forests and monuments, poverty, history repeating itself, and a people striving to succeed against all odds.

I grew up in Manzano, New Mexico at the foot of the beautiful Manzano Mountains which extend Southeast of Albuquerque and South of the Sandia Mountains just one hour from Albuquerque, the largest city in New Mexico. 30 million years ago this New Mexico geographic setting was formed when the bottom fell out of the Rio Grande Valley. The Manzano Mountain range is on the South and the Sandia Mountains on the North. The little Manzanita range links the two. The Sandia's and the Manzanitas are separated by Tijeras Canyon.

From Tramway take I-40 East toward Santa Rosa 6.2 miles, at Exit 175 take ramp Right for NM 337/NM333 toward Tijeras and continue 30 miles. Turn right onto NM-55 toward Mountainair.

Though the destination is Manzano, you will not experience a dull moment on your journey there. The canyon views are spectacular and the road has many switchbacks and curves opening up to aromatic pinon, ponderosa pines, juniper, cedar, fir and oak trees, and various wild flowers. Trails are provided for all levels of hiking and you can enjoy Pine Flats for a day of picnicking. My sister in law Gigi would not attempt the drive without her barf bag and my Brother Eleno screeched to a halt several times to allow her stomach to settle.

On years when the pinon trees are bountiful with nuts you will observe cars and trucks parked on either side of the road. These families are on an outing picking pinon nuts by hand as fast as chickens pick the feed which is strewn for them on the earth. Traditionally families turn this into a full day of work and picnicking. In order to get the nuts still on the cone one places a large tarp on the ground and a strong person climbs the tree in order to shake the branches, and the pinon falls like rain on the tarp and is much faster and easier than picking it from mother earth.   These nuts are taken home, rinsed, dried, and roasted. Now they are ready for eating like a sun flower seed or used when baking. They are also sold by the pound all over New Mexico and yield a nice profit.

The pinon tree excretes Trementina (white sap) which is used for removing a deep splinter under the skin. It also removes pus and boils from an infected area. The trementina is heated until it becomes gummy then applied as one would a patch or poultice. It can also be dried and ground and used on the infected area.

In route to Manzano feast your eyes on numerous small quaint villages; Escobosa, Chilile, Tajique, and Torreon (old Spanish Fort); each town has its own church and unique traditions. It is a common sight during the fall months to see colorful red chile ristras hung from home porches and posts. They have been strung and hung to dry allowing the sun and open breeze to facilitate quick drying which is necessary in order to prevent the inside of the chile pod from becoming contaminated with insects or mold. Now the chiles can be pulled from the stems and stored in a dry place; a gunny sack is commonly used as it allows ventilation but a large covered pot or can works well. The chile pods must remain free from moisture.

Large farms sell the chile in pods, ristras, or powdered form and ship packaged in plastic bags which identify it as mild, medium, or hot and sell to produce markets.

Green chile is harvested in much the same way, however, the most common method for consuming green chile is to eat it fresh or to roast, peel, freeze it or dry it. It can be defrosted and chopped up as a garnish in sandwiches with the famous green chile cheeseburgers being the most common.

There are a great variety of methods for preparing both the red and green chile. New Mexico is famous for its chile. People who have lived in New Mexico make a special trip once a year to purchase chile or will request that it be shipped in dry ice from the Land of Enchantment. Once you have become accustomed to our chile you cannot top it.

Very much like a pinon outing – chile roasting and processing is a joyous family or friend event. Several people do the peeling while others process it by adding garlic and packaging it. Cold beer or wine is consumed all while tasting the fruit of your labor. After the work and clean-up is complete burgers are grilled and the feast begins.

Until 1970, the Manzano church, Our Lady of Sorrows was the Mother church of the parishes in: Abo, La Cienega, Punta de Agua, Torreon, Tajique, Escobosa, Pinos Wells, Lincoln, and surrounding areas in the territorial days.

Current Church

During the month of May the parishioners from the neighboring villages walk in procession carrying the statue of The Blessed Virgin Mary and banners while singing and reciting prayers. Upon reaching Manzano various families set up ornate altars and we walked to these homes in procession prior to entering the church. The distance from Torreon to Manzano is seven miles.

You approach Manzano from the Alto (on high/top) giving one a panoramic view of the village and the Manzano Mountains. The village dates to 1800 and gets its name from the apple orchards that were planted by the Franciscan friars traveling to nearby Indian pueblos. The growth rings on the trees show their age to the 1800's. They are the oldest apple orchards in the United States.

Old Orchard

As children we would jump the fence and steal the delicious yellow apples in spite of our fear of Don Alfredo Romero. He was often at watch with his BB gun in tow. The orchard was next to the Manzano Lake –a small lake in the heart of the town where one can fish, swim, or picnic to this date. The lake is fed from "El Ojo Grande" (the large ojo/spring) a spring gushing forth at the base of Manzano Peak which rises to 10,098 feet near the town.

Manzano Lake with Mountains in Background

On weekends the youth of Manzano walked the dirt road up the hill toward the Ojo in pursuit of meeting up with other young boys and girls, and should you score a date you strolled up the hill to the Ojo. East of the lake was a torreon (defense tower) constructed as a protection against Indian attack.

Capilla Peak Southwest of Manzano with an elevation of 10,608 feet is nearby. We often went there for picnics on holidays. One memorable picnic comes to mind when I was about six years old and The Chavez Family came from Albuquerque to ask for my sister Lala's hand in marriage. Prior to their coming Lala paid Dona Emilia Lajuenesse to give our home a thorough cleaning. Dona Emilia was a slim lady who wore an apron and a scarf tied at the back of her neck. She worked swiftly while she washed the tin ceiling and all the walls. She removed the curtains from the bedrooms and kitchen, washed, and ironed them. I recall she took many little breaks to smoke a cigarette. All the linoleum flooring were left gleaming and I was amazed.

My Father consented to the marriage after meeting and interviewing the parents and their son Raymond. Both families proceeded to celebrate the engagement at Capilla Peak. Should the young lady refuse to accept the proposal it was said that they received "las calabazas" (squash/to flunk) with the meal. That was a polite way of making the girl's wishes understood.

The tradition of asking for the girl's hand in marriage still continues to this day but varies. In Northern New Mexico the custom is for the parents of the groom to compose a letter to present to the parents of the girl.

When our son Paul Anthony had intentions of marrying Marianna (Mari) he put us on notice. He did not know the exact date, time, or place that we were to visit the Bacas and said he would let us know. This request felt awkward and went against our nature. We wanted to, at least, let the Baca's know we were coming. Paul simply would not have it and so I purchased a bottle of wine, a basket, and 6 wine glasses for the occasion. I had them ready along with my camera just waiting for the call from Paul. When the day arrived Paul was with Mari in the N. E. Heights in Albuquerque and they were heading to her parent's home in the South Valley therefore he wanted us to go right then.

Luckily, we were acquainted with the Bacas (Julian and Camilla) from our parish. The four of us were on a team that hosted a Marriage Enrichment Week-end and that made it a little less awkward. We knocked at the door and Mr. Baca greeted us politely, however, they had just said goodbye to out of state relatives and certainly were not prepared for us. I left the wine and glasses in the vehicle while we visited by making small talk. Seemed like forever before Paul and Mari arrived. In reality it was about half an hour. They said hello to the four of us and went into the kitchen and shut the door. Eventually my husband J.M. sat at the edge of the seat and said to Mr. Baca "I hate to interrupt you but we are not here to visit". That really caught their attention. My husband continued "We came here because Paul sent us and it is with great honor that we ask you for Mari's hand in marriage.

The Bacas were shocked- I believe that Celia, Mari's younger sister knew what was happening as she seemed to appear out of thin air. Mari's parents asked Celia to get Paul and Mari from the kitchen. Paul and Mari came into the living room, sat and visited with us. Mari, totally unsuspecting until her Dad got her attention and told her about Paul's request in having us visit them.

Mari looked so beautiful in her white shirt and red jumper and she too was shocked. Her eyes were full of tears and she leaned into Paul's shoulder. Her Father requested an answer and again she cried and leaned into Paul and finally said- Yes. At that point I went to the car to retrieve the wine, glasses, and camera. Camilla, her Mother, brought out a couple of tall candle sticks, we toasted the engaged couple, lit the candles and congratulated them and ourselves as we would become Compadres with the union of our children in marriage.

I have various examples of people requesting "a hand in marriage" and many did not end as beautifully as the one which remains near and dear to my heart but at least I have given you the flavor of a long-standing tradition.

The family home in Manzano sits at the center of the "Y" as NM-55 forks toward Mountainair and the 4th of July and Manzano Campgrounds in the Cibola National Forest. The home dates to the 1800's and is constructed from dual stacked adobes making the outer walls about 24 inches deep. The square footage is approximately 3,500 which was very large for those days. Some unique characteristics of the home are: The huge single door leading into the salon (the hall) 5 feet, 3 inches wide and 8 feet tall with an ornate frame. Above the door are seven small windows and two windows on either side. The salon approximately 20' x 55' is situated in the center of the home and has vigas (beams) on the ceiling. It served as a mercantile store which my Grandfather Eleno operated for many decades in the 1800's.

Main Doorway to Mercantile Store

What we called the main bedroom has a fireplace and a bay window. It too has a decorative frame and measures five feet, four inches. The bay windows opened at the center forming two doors. Here we sat and looked out onto the highway and put on our little concerts and plays when we were children. The home has two dormer windows on the roof. Meat was hung from the rafters to dry (Carne seca/jerky) used for stews, chile or a gourmet snack. It goes without saying that we climbed up into the attic to sneak meat. The very best jerky comes from deer and there were hundreds in the nearby mountains.

The window sills throughout the home were deep which allowed ample space for white, pink, and red geranium pots. In the winter months Lala made jello and placed the bowl overnight to congeal on the window sills, I thought it was magic! All the other rooms in the home have metal ceilings with different patterns. The floors throughout were wide wood planks. The front porch is approximately 50 feet by 8 feet and had several carved posts to set it off. The roof, as long as I can remember, has been tin and was later painted red. The home was probably the finest home in Manzano.

Family Home

On the property sat a well where we drew water for all our household needs and Daddy had a large trough hollowed out from a tree trunk where the animals drank. He also planted corn, pumpkins, and chile on the tract of land, with apple, pear, and peach trees. There were several corrals, two barn houses, a chicken coop, pig pen, and two outhouses. Dad was obsessive about cleanliness, organization, and frugality. I guess you could say we lived the style of "farm to table" which some people think was invented recently.

Barn with Grade School in Background

3 Cuentos, Canciones y Poesia
Tales, Songs, and Poems

I feel fortunate to have grown up with such rich culture and to have experienced old traditions including visiting friends, relatives, and neighbors which involved music and storytelling. In addition, living in a part of the state with ancient surroundings, nearby lake, mountains, state parks, and national monuments was a plus.

The people from Punta de Agua and Quarai attended mass in Manzano and the children from those villages were bused to school in Mountainair with us. This resulted in Dad making the acquaintance of people from these villages, therefore, Dad had friends to visit in both those places. While the adults visited indoors at the Luna home, we children played in the red-walled ruins of Quarai. Onate first approached this thriving pueblo in 1598 to accept its oath of allegiance to Spain.

Quarai Ruins

I returned to Quarai as an adult in 1997 with my sisters Cecilia, Candie and two childhood friends from Manzano. We went there for the purpose of attending a concert held in the ruins with guest performer Roberto A. Mondragon. In 1966 at the age of 25 Roberto was appointed to the legislature and he was approached by the Sgt. at Arms Amadeo Lucero who was a retired school teacher after 36 years. Mr. Lucero was a song and story writer and he asked Mr. Mondragon to introduce a bill to the House and Senate which would make his song "Asi Es Nuevo Mexico the official New Mexico State song. The song was enthusiastically received and promptly adopted. The lyrics and literal English translation can be uploaded on You-Tube.

Up to that point New Mexico only had an English version of a state song. It was "O Fair New Mexico" written by Elizabeth Garrett in 1917; she was the blind daughter of the famed Pat Garrett who killed Billy the Kid. It is said that New Mexican children were forced by teachers to memorize the lyrics although it did not reflect Spanish American culture. Roberto A. Mondragon later served as Lieutenant Governor of New Mexico from 1971 – 1983 under 2 administrations. Mr. Mondragon is a New Mexico treasure in that he is an activist, musician, politician, song composer, singer, and helps preserve and maintain the Hispanic Heritage of New Mexico.

That concert was particularly meaningful, spiritual, and healing for me. I had lost my son Joseph at 25 years old in August 1996 and my emotions were very raw. Listening to the songs in such a spectacular setting in the open space with great acoustics was powerful. I removed myself from my group and must have cried the entire concert. It appears to me that happiness and sorrow are so close an emotion. I listen to the songs that make me happy and can't help but remembering all the wonderful times I have shared with loved ones - which in turn make me sad.

Allow yourself ample time to visit the charming historic Shaffer Hotel which was built in 1920. It is located in Mountainair at 103 West Main only 6 miles from Quarai and a perfect respite especially if you are continuing on to Gran Quivira. The hotel has a dining room with an adjoining gift shop and art gallery. The atmosphere is relaxed with excellent food and is reasonably priced. The architectural features are unique with animal shaped wood chandeliers and Native American exteriors. Currently 17 rooms have been refurbished for overnight lodging.

Shaffer Hotel

Shaffer Hotel Wood Chandeliers

Gran Quivira (also known as Las Humanas) is the largest of the Salinas Pueblos and was an important trade center for many years before and after the Spanish entered. Artifacts from the site are proof of Spanish presence and is reflected in the pueblo's black-on-white pottery which reflects European styles. In addition, Chinese porcelain, metal tools, religious medallions, and evidence of cattle, goats, sheep, horses and pigs have been found. Documents from the 1600's tell of strife between missionaries and the encomenderos, who complained that the friars kept the Indians so busy studying Christianity and building churches that the encomenderos could not use Indian labor nor collect their tributes. In the 1660's friars burned and filled kivas in an effort to exterminate the old religion.

Gran Quivira Ruins

Cuentos (stories), canciones (songs) and poems (poesia) instruct, delight, and recreate moments which the Spanish settlers experienced. They evoke the wisdom, customs, and values of the time. The main impulse is to create a meaningful world with language. Some were shared purely for fun and range from tales about witches, devils, clever animals, etc.

I remember as a child visiting two Candelaria brothers. I visited them with   my Father where we sat around a wood burning stove with a pot of coffee perking while they talked, which felt to me like forever. They shared stories in a small smoke-filled room with a kerosene lamp as the light source. One of the brothers had the knack for telling outrageous stories. One story was about an old lady, though I don't remember the punchline, I do recall what he did while telling it. First he broke two wooden match sticks, next he formed a fist and placed the heads of the matches between his fingers - they became the old ladies' eyes, the knuckle of the middle finger below became the nose, next he got the top of a bottle cap - that was the mouth/teeth and finally he pulled a red handkerchief from his pocket and wrapped it like a scarf- that framed the old ladies face. His fingers were old and crooked with arthritis and that frightened me. Good story tellers created a spell in the room and filled a void by bringing entertainment.

In 1966 Cargo ran for governor of New Mexico and my Father composed a corrido as a tribute to him. He then commissioned two musicians to join us at a recording studio in Albuquerque. We had several records made and later drove to the state capitol in Santa Fe where we proudly presented a record to Governor David Cargo. He gave us an autographed 8" x 10" photograph of himself and we returned home happy as larks.

These traditions had an impact on me. As an adult I wrote a corrido about my Father when he was 93 and nearing his end of life. As I was singing, playing my guitar, and attempting to put words to music I shed many a tear while reflecting on what my Father meant to me. It is my opinion that the technology of today has taken away from our youth the ability/art of socializing verbally. They need to be entertained and amused by an outside source. The following is the song about my Father Santiago which I composed.

Adios Daddy
Farewell Daddy

Adios con el Corazon, que con el alma no	Goodbye I say with my heart, I can not
Puedo, Al despedirme de ti, al despedirme	offer my soul. To say farewell to you
Me muero.	Really pains me.

Fuiste tu mi madre y mi padre, mi amigo
Y mi doctor, siempre fuiste mi companero
Y en cambio ganaste todo mi amor

You have been my Father and Mother
my companion and my confidant.
You have been my nurse and my doctor and In turn have earned all of my love

Me llevaste contigo a la iglesia

Me ensenaste resar oraciones, Me ensenaste

Cantar alabados, Y ahora te alabo
Con mis versos.

You took me with you to the temple, and
taught me to recite my prayers. You taught me to sing holy praises and now
I praise you Daddy

With these verses.

Tu sufriste mucho en esta vida Y cargaste
Muchos Dolores, valla Daddy con el padre

Eterno Y vive feliz en la Gloria eternal

You have suffered much in this life and
have carried many a burden. Go now Dad with our Holy Father
and live on with Him a life everlasting.

Ahoy nos despidemos de ti

Pero en nuestro pensamiente tu sigues
Resando Y alabando a Dios

Que fue el ejemplo que tu nos diste

Today we say farewell to you, but in our
hearts you live on. Singing praises
praying to God which is the example you
left us.

Tus eras el bien de mi vida, tu seras el
Bien de mi alma. Tu seras el pajaro pinto
Que allegre canta por la manana

You have been the good in my life. You'll
remain the good in my soul. You will be
the spotted bird singing joyfully as I awake in the early morning.

Only 9 miles from Mountainair are the Abo Ruins which date to the 14th century.   Abo was a thriving community when the Spaniards visited in 1581. Nearby salt deposits afforded residents of this valley a valuable commodity to trade with other nearby tribes or the Great Plains Indians. The Franciscans began converting Abo residents to Catholicism in 1622 and the first church was completed in the late 1620's. The natives left between 1671 –1678 to take refuge in towns along the Rio Grande.

As with all historic areas administered by the National Park Service, the Abo ruins were listed on the National Register of Historic Places on Oct. 15, 1966.
While visiting the ruins I had the privilege of meeting and visiting Eliseo and Ernestine Sisneros who live in their ancestral home on the grounds. In 1938 the State of New Mexico acquired the ruins and surrounding property from the Sisneros family. The National Park Service took over the ruins in 1981 and incorporated Abo, Quarai, and Gran Quivira Ruins together into what is now known as the Salinas Pueblo Missions.

Abo Ruins

The Sisneros were able to keep several acres and have remained in their beloved residence which sits on the grounds where the ruins are located.

An older gentleman Don Ponceano Sanchez was a friend of Dad's whom we visited in Abo. I thought him to be extremely intelligent as he was able to recite poems and dichos from memory. The Sisneros' directed me to Don Ponceano's home and were in agreement with me that he was in fact brilliant and a very interesting individual. The following is a poem he wrote about Manzano.

Old Ponceano House

Recuerdos De Manzano
Remembering Manzano

How beautiful is Manzano
With its mountains, gardens and orchards

Que bonito es el Manzano
con montes, huertas y arboledas

Though residents live out of the way	aun que vivan en fronteras
They have a joyful life	todos han de vivir gustosos
The land is fruitful,	porque todo el terreno es frondoso[
just and beautiful.	Justamente y bonito
I saw it leisurely	yo lo vi con despacito
And can say with certainty	y digo de aqui a la mano
That all its citizens have had	que cualquier ciudadano
A thousand advantages	de los que alla estan viviendo
How beautiful is Manzano	mil ventajas han tenido
	Que bonito es el Manzano
I repeat that Manzano	Repito que es el Manzano
Is a great place to live and can also tell you	buen lugar para vivir
They enjoy crystalline waters	y tambien les se decir
There the neighbors see	que usan aguas cristalinas
Each other as brothers	alli se ven las vecinas
And I repeat to you once more	y vecinos como hermanos
How beautiful is Manzano	y les vuelvo a repetir
	Que bonito es el Manzano
Its mountain range is beautiful	Su sierrania es hermosa
During the summer season	en la estacion del verano
Crystalline are its streams	cristalinas son sus aguas
Which reach out to Manzano	que llegan hasta el Manzano
They sweeten the memories	dulcifican los recuerdos
Of the ancient settlers	de los primeros ancianos
Who with great sacrifice	que con grande sacrificio
Populated this Manzano	poblaron ese Manzano
An apple orchard grows	Alli esta una arboleda

there

Which dates back three hundred years	que cuenta trecientos anos
You can find choke cherry and plums	hay capulin y ciruela
In the Manzano fields	en los prados del Manzano
It's a prehistoric place	es prehistorico el lugar
For all its citizens	para todo ciudadano
And once more I repeat	y les vuelvo a repetir
How beautiful is Manzano	que bonito es el Manzano

There is a clear spring	Alli esta un ojo de agua
Which is a precious thing	lo cual es cosa preciosa
Here you may see butterflies	alli se ven mariposas
In the summer season	en la estacion del verano
The citizens divert themselves	se divierte el ciudadano
With what they see	tan solo de ver las cosas
Carnations and roses appear	se ven claveles y rosas
How beautiful is Manzano	que bonito es el Manzano

How beautiful is Manzano	Que bonito es el Manzano
You must admire its allure	amirable su belleza
Crystalline are the waters	cristalinas son las aguas
That are deposited at the dam	que deposita la presa
Which our forefathers	que nuestros parimeros padres
With much vigor and toil	con todo vigor y fuerza
Left to us as an inheritance	nos dejaron como herencia
In this sovereign place	en ese lugar soberano
And I repeat with love	y repito con carino
How beautiful is Manzano	que bonito es el Manzano

There my mother was born	Alli mi madre nacio
In that lovely place	en ese lugar hermoso
It's forests were lush	sus bosques son frondosos

I remember as a child	me recuerdo cuando nino
Though it has all passed	anque ya todo paso
As summer passes	como se pasa el verano
I must say with love	pero siempre con carino
How beautiful is Manzano	que bonito es el Manzano
Manzano was my cradle	El Manzano fue mi cuna
There I was born	alli fue mi nacimiento
There I received Baptism	alli recivi el sacramento
As God's creature	como toda un criatura
At this moment I will say	y en el momento dire
With opportune phrases	con frases muy oportunas
That Manzano was the cradle	que el Manzano fue la cuna
Of my joyful birth	de mi feliz nacimiento
And again I repeat	y repito en el momento
How beautiful is Manzano	que bonito es el Manzano
There live my friends	Alli estan las amistades
That I acquired as a child	que granjie cuando era nino
There they view me with love	alli me ven con carino
Friends, cousins and brothers	amigos, primos y hermanos
For this I live with gratitude	de esto vivo agradecido
And I extend my hand with love	y les extiendo la mano repitiendo con carino
How beautiful is Manzano	Que bonito es el Manzano
With this I bid thee farewell	Ya con esto me despido
I took the pen in my hand	tomo le pluma en la mano
To write down these verses	para anotarle estos versos
To the village of Manzano	a la plaza de Manzano
If someone asks who is the author	si preguntan por el autor

Tell them it is Don Ponciano	que es Don Ponciano
A resident of Abo	un residente de Abo
Born in Manzano	y residente rn el Manzano
I entrust to the lectors	Les encargo a los lectores
That they must reflect	que tienen que reflejar
If in some way I was	si en algo me he equivocado
Mistaken they must forgive me	me tienen que dispensar
For every branch has its threads	por que no hay palo sin hebra
And God is the final word.	Solo Dios es cabal

Buenos dias le de Dios (God grant you a good day). This is how I was taught as a child to greet my elders. It is a greeting of respect, a cultural value, one that has been passed on through the generations.

The old people I remember from my childhood were strong in their faith, recognized the design of creation and were a God-fearing people. Everything in the village revolved around the church i.e.: baptism, confirmation, stations of the cross, rosaries, benediction, catechism class, pre-marriage classes, confessions, wakes, novenas, sodality clubs for the young adults. There were masses for the dead, the patron saint, the sick, the fiestas, graduations, Sundays, Lent, midnight mass, Christmas, Easter, and days of obligation.

I can't leave the subject of the influence of the Church in our daily lives without mentioning the tremendous role that altar boys played in Church rituals. Today the job of altar boys has evolved into an almost ornamental practice. When I was growing up in the 50's and 60's the altar boys played a vital function. A considerable amount of training was required, uppermost of which was the memorization of the many Latin prayers that they recited throughout the Mass. Before Mass even started the altar boys would light the altar candles designating a low or a High Mass. They assisted the priest in the washing of hands and moving the scripture books to the proper place on the altar. At solemn times they carried the censer for burning incense which lent a mystical feeling to the services with all the aromatic smoke billowing throughout the church. They rang the bells during the Sanctus, the Consecration and Lamb of God portions of the service. Before the Blessed Sacrament was distributed the altar boys would lift a cover over the altar railing so the congregation could place their folded hands under the cloth as they knelt to receive the Eucharist. The altar boy would hold the paten under the communicant's chin should the sacred host fall. I can't overemphasize the reverence which was given to the precious host. It was a definite taboo for a lay person to touch the host with anything but their tongue. There were many other functions the altar boys performed depending on which service was taking place, i.e. Stations of the Cross, funerals, baptisms, weddings, or memorial services, but suffice it to say that their actions were much more extensive than today and added a great deal of flair to the solemnity of the services. We have lost a lot of the mystique surrounding Church services in our "enlightened" period. One of the few rewards which altar boys received was when they were fortunate enough to serve at a wedding or sometimes at a funeral Mass. At a wedding the altar boys would go to congratulate the couple and the groom would usually reward them with as much as a $5.00 bill.

One of my closest friends was my cousin Stella Silva whose father was mother's relative. Tio (uncle) Santos was completely deaf yet he seemed to have an invisible leash on us. Should we stray too far from the property or attempt to start a fire which might endanger us – there he appeared and simply gestured for us to Stop! To say he was a man of few words would be an exaggeration, for I never heard him speak at all. On the opposite side of the coin was his wife, Tia Carmelita who was very animated, with various engagements away from the home, and was a multi-tasker if I ever saw one. I came from our quiet, orderly home, where Dad with his authoritative tone had no need to raise his voice and we did as he commanded, to Tia's who felt the need to raise her voice to get our attention i.e.; don't sit on the sofa, don't break the records, I just cleaned that room, put that away, etc. I recall thinking "I am glad I don't have a Mom" and have to be subjected to this nagging. At the same time, she allowed us plenty of freedom and I and all my siblings loved her. She would abruptly leave the home to attend a rosary, a novena or clean the church leaving the bread dough to rise, the ironing half done, or the broom and dust pan in the center of the kitchen. Today I find myself doing much the same and find that those unfinished projects wait on me. She was a pillar in the community and orchestrated much of what was done in regards to cleaning the church, laundering/starching the altar linens, and ensuring that the priest's vestments were impeccable. It appears she was in control of the choir members and altar servers as well. She and other women in the altar society were in charge of cleaning both the church and the priest's home.

Her sister, Mi Madrina (God mother) Libradita confirmed me and she assisted Tia Carmelita in everything at church. Madrina Libradita's personality was starkly different, being the quiet and pious one. She lived about one city block from the church and made frequent visits to the church throughout the day with her rosary and prayer book in tow. Apparently, she had a whole lot to pray about. In those days a mantilla (head covering) or hat was essential for women to wear when in the church. There were variations ranging from silk scarfs, ornate black shoulder lengths ones, to a simple round one that covered only the top of the scalp which is what the young girls wore. It seems rather odd to me that women must cover their heads while men were required to uncover their heads when entering church.

My Madrina just could not shower me with enough love; she waited for me to exit mass in order to hug and kiss me over and over and it continued when I matured and married.

Stella had a younger brother named Michael who insisted on being a choir member in the day when the choir consisted of only girls and we simply did not want to make room for him. Tia Carmelita stepped in and ordered that he in fact be allowed. This darn kid taught himself to play the organ and became our leader. He made quite a name for himself as he wrote lyrics and composed music for masses and was in demand to sing and play at funerals, weddings, and various other events. His songs were frequently requested to be played on the radio and continued to be requested years after his death.

Men also had their distinct duties including cleaning the grounds, digging graves, doing needed repairs to the church and the rectory, as well as ushering and ringing the church bells to announce the beginning of services. According to Orlando Lopez there was a distinct method of ringing the bells which conveyed different messages such as High Mass, announcing the death of a parishioner, processions or other events.
Should any of these activities take place after dark the whole town knew that Don Zamora, our Dad would be watching for his children with a bright flash light prepared to escort us home. It was an embarrassment for us.

Our Lady of Sorrows 2020

Nuestra Senora de Los Dolores (Our Lady of Sorrows) has had a long past and still continues serving as a hub when services are held. It was built in 1829 after Tome, N.M. citizens were granted license by Vicar Rascon to build a place of worship. Archbishop Jean Baptiste Lamy assigned his nephew to serve in the mid 1870's and Rev. Anthony Lamy served from 1874 – 1876. He is buried at the foot of the altar inside the church. Father Roberto Garrassu who died June 02, 1897 another priest assigned to the parish is also buried at the foot of the altar.

I have been told that the bell was made by The Meneely Andrew Foundry which existed in 1826 in West Troy, New York. The Meneely Foundry made over 65,000 bells which were shipped all over many states. The business closed in 1952 after three generations.

There have been many faithful and devoted parishioners including many of my ancestors. Prior to 1821, under Spanish rule, commercial trade was restricted to merchandise obtained via the Camino Real (Royal Road) between Santa Fe, New Mexico and Chihuahua, Mexico. With Mexican independence from Spain, trade continued along El Camino Real but was expanded to include goods brought over the Santa Fe Trail between St Louis, Missouri and Santa Fe.

The Zamora family came to Manzano in the 1800's. They lived side by side, sharing, growing together and they knew the rhythms and cycles of time, from preparation of the earth in the spring to the digging of the acequias (irrigation ditches) which provided water for the crops.

The following chapters are the Zamora family genealogy of that time period:

Born 1811 – Great Grandfather Jose' de Jesus Blas
             Zamora
Born 1814 – Great Grandmother Isabelita Maldonado
             Zamora Archuleta
Born 1830 - Step Great Grandfather Juan Jose Archuleta
             *2nd husband

Born 1845 – Our Grandfather Eleno Zamora
Born 1850 – Grandmother Anastacia Chavez Zamora
             *1st wife
Born 1866 - Our Grandmother Vicenta Gacia Zamora
             *2nd wife

4 The Colorful life of my Great Grandfather
Jose' de Jesus Blas Zamora
Born January 11, 1811

Jose' de Jesus Blas was born in Tome, New Mexico, South of Albuquerque, New Mexico to Juan Andres Zamora and Maria Petra Dolores Baca. When he was a young boy of 10 the Mexican Government granted Juan Andres, his Father, a strip of land along the river in the fertile, colorful village of Casa Colorada. While working alongside his Father and learning farming he attended school where he learned to read and write.

At the age of 23 he married Isabela Maldonado on April 22, 1834. She was 20 years old and born in Tome, New Mexico in 1814 to Manuel Maldonado and Maria Josefa Ruiz.

It was 11 years later that they actually begun their family. During that time Great Grandmother Isabela gave birth 4 times, and each time the babies died at infancy. Eventually they had 4 children:

    Our Grandfather – Eleno Born 1845
                      Manuel Born 1847
                      Maria de la Paz 1854
                      Lucas 1856

My Great Grandfather Jose' de Jesus Blas earned a living by hauling agricultural products to the region of Rio Bonito in Lincoln County and to Las Vegas, New Mexico. Eventually he prospered and became very successful. He also dealt in the trade and purchase of animal skins. It is said that he was industrious, hardworking, and brave, however, he was "Hot Headed" and hateful. While lodging overnight, in route to deliveries he frequented bars where he drank heavily and engaged in card games where he got into physical altercations which at times involved knives and guns. It was during one of those brawls at a bar in Manzano, New Mexico that his life came to an abrupt end at the age of 47.

Several days after this incident his corpse was transported to Casa Colorada where he was claimed by his family. He was buried at the church cemetery there on June 01, 1858.

5 Great Grandmother – The Green-Eyed Beauty
Isabelita Maldonado, Zamora, Archuleta
Born 1814

Her parents were Manuel Maldonado and Maria Josefa Ruiz. She did not attend school and never learned to read or write. She married my Great Grandfather Jose' de Jesus Blas Zamora at 20 years of age.

It is said that she was a green-eyed beauty with very light skin and hair. (our sister Cecilia Zamora Bachicha has those characteristics). Many of our people, wanting to feel a part of the dominant Anglo-Saxon establishment, felt it was desirable to have "white" features. Having said that, one can only imagine how she felt to be 44 years old and a widow with 4 children ages 13, 11, 4, and 2 to raise and support. After the death of her husband Jesus Blas she left her home in Casa Colorada, South of Belen and moved her family to live in the prosperous village of Manzano where she sought the assistance of relatives. They made their home in a very small shack/hut that was located behind her sisters' home. The sister that aided Great Grandmother Isabela (my father called her Isabelita) was Apolinaria Maldonado Otero and her husband Pedro Otero.

It is my observation that much is known and recounted about the males of those times. Fewer details are recorded about the females, yet as one inquires often times the women were the back bone of the family, the survivors (the wind beneath the wings). Many women sold their hand-crafted wares, their preserves, breads, goat, and cow cheeses and yogurt. They were extremely resourceful, thrifty, and recycled items such as fabric from flour sacks which they used to fashion clothing for their large families. They made bedding for the family stuffing cotton batting with straw and later with cotton. Their husbands were away (the hunters and gatherers) much of the time leaving the females to run the household.

Two (2) years after the death of husband Jose' de Jesus Blas she ended her "luto" (a Spanish word meaning mourning where women wore only black) and remarried in Manzano at age 46 to Juan Jose' Archuleta on November 09, 1860. She gave birth to a daughter whom they baptized on April 01, 1861.

Great Grandmother Isabela died a sudden death at age 87 and was laid to rest in the Manzano cemetery on October 13, 1901.

6 The Adventurous Stepfather
Juan Jose Archuleta
Born 1830

Don Jose Archuleta was the 2nd husband to our Great Grandmother Isabela Zamora. They married on November 09, 1860 just 2 years after the death of her first husband Jose' de Jesus Blas Zamora.

Juan Jose became the stepfather to;
> My Grandfather Eleno - Born 1845
> Manuel - Born 1847
> Maria de la Paz - Born 1854
> Lucas - Born 1856

My Father Santiago Zamora spoke very highly and lovingly about these aunts and uncles of his. They all passed prior to my birth.

Juan Jose's physical stature was compared to that of an enormous bear. His occupations varied. He transported a variety of products ie. dry goods, animal skins, household items, animal pelts, etc. In addition, he had the reputation for being one of the most renowned hunters in the region and was an accurate shot. He was a trapper of bears, mountain lions, lobos, mountain goats, and beavers. He hiked to the very top of the Manzano Mountains in pursuit of trophy game. He wore all leather attire with fringe, a leather cap with a hanging raccoon tail, and moccasins for foot wear.

Once a year Juan Jose' mounted his horse and led a group of men to hunt herds of thousands of buffalo which roamed and grazed the hills close to Fort Stanton and Puerto de Luna.

On horse and wagon periodically, he transported a cargo of animal skins/pelts to St. Louis, Missouri. There he exchanged goods for lamp oil, hardware goods, and various types of fabric. One trip took 10 months to complete. Only the most adventurous and brave men were to pursue this journey as it was dangerous. They encountered raids by Apache and Navajo Indians and terrible wind/snow storms and illnesses.

Don Juan Jose' also organized platoons of villagers and led punitive guerrilla warfare expeditions against Indian tribes. He was not one to be crossed as he would take revenge to the point of death. His reputation ranged from: bravery, success, drunkenness, quick to anger, abrasive, and cruelty to the point of beating his children with an iron rod.

He found himself an elderly widower, ill. and frail to the point that he could no longer care for himself. He was taken in by his step-son Tio Lucas Zamora and his wife Porfiria who cared for him. The census of 1910 records that he did not read or write. He passed away in Manzano at 87 years of age and was buried on July 26, 1917 in the village cemetery.

7 The Staunch Entrepreneur Grandfather
Eleno Zamora
Born 1845

Grandfather Eleno was born in Casa Colorada, New Mexico, the eldest son of Jose de Jesus Blas Zamora and Maria Isabela Maldonado. After the unfortunate death of his Father Jose de Jesus Blas his Mother Isabelita took her family; Grandfather Eleno oldest, Manuel, Maria de la Paz, and Lucas to live in Manzano where she had family members. Grandfather Eleno, now the man of the house at 13 took on work with ranchers and farmers in the region to help support the family.

2 years after his Fathers' death his Mother Isabelita married Don Jose Archuleta. My Dad remembers stories from his Father Eleno telling that Don Jose was brutal, dominating, and took to beating them with a metal rod. It is no wonder that Eleno chose to pack his belongings and flee to begin a new life for himself in Santa Fe, N.M. at the age of 15. One year later, he lied about his age, and in 1861 he enlisted in the military with the Union American Services. He fought during the war against the states, The Civil War. He served honorably and was promoted to corporal. During his time in service he was injured twice while in combat and was subsequently discharged with honors in 1866. He received a government pension as the result of injuries to hand and ribs. Grandfather Eleno returned to Santa Fe after his military service and found employment as a fletero (carrier of freight/cargo) and eventually store manager.

In 1868 at 23 he married Anastacia Chavez (BD1850)
who was born in Santa Fe and was the daughter of
Francisca Chavez. They had 4 children;

> Maria BD1870
> Rosarito BD 1873
> Isabelita BD1876
> Nicolas BD1879

Anastacia passed away suddenly 13 years later, at age
31. Three years after his wife passed he returned, a
widower at age 37, to his childhood home of Manzano
with his 4 children in tow. He sought to open his own
store with the financial backing from his former employer
Charles Ilfield. He ran a very successful business over 40
years. He was admired by everyone in the community
and the region and was known to be astute at business,
honest, stern, sincere, and pious.

At 45 years of age he married Vicenta Garcia, 21 years
his junior, on May 19, 1890. She was born in El Sausal
on May 30, 1866 to Ignacio Garcia and Dolores Padilla.
Grandfather Eleno and Grandmother Vicenta had 9
children:

> Manuel BD1892
> Francisquita BD1893
> Mercedes 1894
> Anita BD1896
> Ignacio BD1898
> Casimiro BD1900
> Santiago BD1902 – Our Father
> Antonio BD1904
> Ramona BD1904

Now they had a blended family of 13.

Grandpa Eleno

In his mercantile store he sold beans, potatoes, large
cans of fruits, hard candy kept in barrels, flour, sugar,

and grains which were weighed on a large scale and sold by the pound. He also sold dry goods ie; clothing, fabric and hardware goods. He treated his loyal customers with respect and rewarded them with an extra scoop of flour, sugar, or a couple cans of fruit. He sent those customers home with a paper sack full of hard candies for their children. The store had a long counter which he marked with thumb tacks used to measure out the distance of one yard of fabric which was brought in by the bolt. At times, he took trade in lieu of cash and accepted gold coins. Don Reyes Salas traded with gold coins which were weighed by the ounce and came in different sizes. Dad recalls an old metal trunk with cash and coins having $5,000.00 at any given time. Grandfather Eleno would not use a bank.

While he did extend credit to customers, he refused credit accounts to clients as he saw fit and especially if he knew they had traded elsewhere. Quote "You go there with cash and come here asking for credit". One client said "I'll go to Tabet's, I don't need you", Grandfather challenged him "I bet he won't trust you either" and a fight ensued. The Tabets owned a competing mercantile store in Manzano. Many Tabets who emigrated from Lebanon came to Manzano mountain communities because the people were kind, accepting and welcomed outside people among them. The Spanish and Arab people had a long history in Spain which made it easier for them to assimilate into our communities.

During this period timber for railroad ties were being harvested near Manzano and several saw mills were operating in the area. The influx of workers at these saw mills contributed to the success of my Grandfather's as well as the Tabets' mercantile business. The Tabets eventually opened a store in Mountainair and established businesses in Belen where to this day these have blossomed into tremendously successful enterprises.

He managed his business with prudence, strict routine and his family as though it were a business as well. He was of medium height, fair skinned, light eyes, slightly over- weight, and partially bald. In his senior years his hair was white and he grew a large mustache. He dressed in business attire; a tie, light shirt, suit jacket, and a hat. He was a formal man, his voice was loud and harsh, he spoke slowly, and distinctly. He used a strict tone when speaking to the children and his wife Vicenta and they all feared him.

On the plot where the store/home sat (still sits 2020) is a triangle piece, where he harvested a vegetable garden. He acquired several hundred acres of land where he raised cattle, sheep, pigs and his beloved beautiful race horses. In the field he planted a huge amount of beans, grains, potatoes, etc. When harvest time came, he traveled to Arroyo Colorado, a village 4-5 miles from Manzano to hire 10-12 men to help in harvesting. All the work was done manually.

When it came time to butchering a cow or pig, he never failed to send a large slab of meat to his first set of children, (the children from his first wife Anastacia). Upon hearing of the butchering neighbors would send their children to purchase 10 cents worth of meat. Grandfather Eleno would ask "What can a dime buy you"? He then proceeded to carve out a large portion to feed the family size and gave it to them free of charge. Therefore, after the butchering was over – most of the meat was also over (gone).

Every year he fattened 3 of the large pigs. He was meticulous in the care of his pigs and horses. Prior to feeding the pigs the trochil (receptacle) had to be scrubbed thoroughly using a gunny sack. In addition to scraps given for food he made a "Salvo" to keep them healthy and well nourished. The pigs provided the family with pork and enough lard to last the year for cooking meals. The horses too were special and he knew exactly when they were to give birth. He made a bed using old blankets for them to rest on and stayed the night with them if he saw it necessary. His horses were a source of pride for him. Once his son Casimiro took one of the horses to El Chato near Manzano, turns out some horse racing was going on. Severo Pena's horse had won the last race and a friend of Casimiro requested to borrow Grandpas horse for the following race. Sure enough, he loaned his horse and the horse won! Later, by accident, Grandfather Eleno heard about the race from a friend who praised Grandfather Eleno on his fast horse that won at the horse races. Now Casimiro was in trouble and his Father tied him up with a rope to ready him for a beating - fortunately he was able to release himself and run.

One day Grandfather Eleno allowed his daughters, my Aunts, Mercedes and Francisquita to ride 2 horses. Apparently, they met a couple of young men who were out riding horses as well and the 4 rode together. When Grandfather got wind of what occurred he took the girls to the barn, wound their hands with a rope and hung them by their wrists to a beam for a good while

Another time, Dad recalls, he sent his sons Casimiro and Ignacio for wood in the forest of the Manzanos and apparently, they overloaded the wagon which made the load too heavy when climbing up hill. This caused the horses to act erratically and free themselves loose. When Grandfather Eleno found out he beat them with a whip and strapped a heavy log to them which they had to pull.

The Census of 1910 reports Grandfather Eleno as a man who could not read or write. My Father, Santiago confirms that. His Dad would sit him for long periods and make him read every last word of the newspaper to him. Dad wonders how his Father was capable of handling a business. Furthermore, Dad said that Grandfather Eleno could run circles around the most educated men when it came to subtraction, addition, and multiplication. He devised a system for himself where he drew small lines, dashes, and dots enabling him to arrive at an answer swiftly. While he had no formal schooling, he could read and write somewhat.

Grandfather Eleno Zamora died a rich man, A ledger left in the store shows thousands of dollars owed him by his customers which were never collected. He died at 79 years of age and was buried in the church cemetery on August 10, 1924.

8 Gentle Grandmother/Stepmother
Vicenta Garcia Zamora

Grandmother Vicenta was born in El Sausal, New Mexico May 30, 1866 to Ignacio Garcia and Dolores Padilla. My Grandfather Eleno asked her parents for her hand in marriage; therefore, it was an arranged marriage which was common in those years. She was 21 years his junior. Grandfather Eleno came with a ready- made family; Maria 20, Rosarito 17, Isabelita 14 and Nicolas 11. Grandfather Eleno had been a widower for 8 years when he returned from Santa Fe, New Mexico to his childhood home of Manzano. His former employer loaned financial support for him to establish his own mercantile store. It was located in the large family home of his youth.

It had to have been a great adjustment to find herself a new bride with a very assertive husband and 4 young step-children, the oldest, Maria, only 1 year her junior. Never-the-less in 1892 only 2 years into married life, she gave birth to the first of 9 more children: Manuel 1892, Francisquita 1893, Mercedes 1894, Anita 1896, Ignacio 1898, Casimiro 1900, Santiago 1902(my Father), Antonio 1904, and Ramona 1904. All these births took place in a span of 12 years. Now the combined sets of kids totaled 13.

I haven't been able to find out too much about Grandmother Vicenta's life. What I know is from my Father Santiago, my sister Frances, and Virginia Romero my 1st cousin. Everyone describes her as very kind hearted and level headed. Two examples of kindness come to mind from my Father. Background; Daddy (Santiago) was visually challenged from youth. He dreaded going to school. In those days 3 students sat side-by- side on a small bench. In order to see the writing on the chalk board, he needed to sit alone as close to the front of the class room as possible. His classmates took to calling him "la gallina ciega" the blind chicken. Daddy figured a way out of his predicament; he would sit next to another child and copy his/her work, however, that backfired. Now he was reprimanded by the teacher who drew a circle on the chalk board and had him place his nose in the circle and remain there. (This too brought bullying). When his Father Eleno found out about him copying from classmates he too punished him and insisted that Daddy read the newspaper aloud to him from cover-to- cover. Daddy says he suffered "las incomparables" the incomparable.

Although Grandfather Eleno owned a thriving mercantile store he refused to have Daddy fitted for glasses. That is when his Mother Vicenta stepped up. Turns out she hid coins from her husband in a little black purse which she carried pinned to her long slip under her skirt. With her own money she purchased his first pair of glasses when he was 10 years old.

Another story from my sister Frances: One Christmas morning when she was a child, she awoke to find a porcelain doll standing near the wood burning stove. It was a gift from Grandmother Vicenta. That was the first real doll Frances ever had. Frances was the oldest Grandchild born to my Father Santiago and Mother Carmen.

Frances can visualize Grandmother lifting her long black skirt to warm her behind on the wood burning stove situated in the center of the room.

After the death of her Husband, Grandfather Eleno in 1924 she continued to live in the family home in Manzano although the store was closed. My Father Santiago and Mother Carmen with their family lived on one side of the house and Grandmother lived on the opposite side which were separated by a large, long salon (hall), where the store had been. My deceased Brother, Eleno joked "we lived in a townhome before they became popular".

In 1940 Grandmother Vicenta left Manzano and relocated in Estancia, New Mexico to live with My Aunt Mercedes and her Husband Tomas Lucero and their family. Her Granddaughters Virginia and Bessie did not appreciate the fact that Grandmother Vicenta would scold her daughter Mercedes for allowing the girls to attend functions outside of the home.

The home at Manzano was given to my Dad Santiago and his brother Ignacio. Eventually our Dad bought Ignacio out and we continued to inhabit the home.

Grandmother Vicenta is remembered to be about 5 feet tall, with dark eyes and hair. Her skin was light and she wore a lot of black, especially her ankle length skirts. She wore black ankle height boots and was not able to read and write. She attended daily mass and walked to church in the center of the road. When a car was coming, she refused to move- saying "I was here first, let them move" Grandmother Vicenta lived to the age of 81 and was buried on March 19, 1947.

Grandmother Vicenta

9 Pobres Huerfanas
Poor Orphans

My Parents Santiago and Carmelita had 10 children and Mother passed when Christela was 7 and I was 3 years old. The two of us plus Lala, and Candie for a short time, were home with Dad. By this time my older siblings had relocated to make their living in Albuquerque. Our older sisters took on the role of housekeeping and mothering. They tended to cooking, laundry, and keeping us well groomed. We complained when they combed us; "Daddy, esta halando mi cabello" (she is pulling my hair). Our hair was very long and they braided it tightly every morning to the point that we resembled Asian children. For special occasions they made up our hair in risos (ringlets). This was done by cutting many long strips of cotton (an old sheet) and wrapping small sections of our hair around the cloth strip, then wrapping the cloth again over the hair and then tied the two ends at the top. The next morning, we had beautiful ringlets.

Christela and I accompanied Dad on all his endeavors including visiting family, friends, and grocery shopping. The poor man was saddled with us. Tabet's Grocery store in Mountainair had an adjoining bar and liquor store separated by a large window. On the first of the month Dad enjoyed a glass of wine while conversing with other men. He gave us money for a soda and candy bar with the understanding that we remain near the window where he could keep an eye on us. We spent our time waving at him and acting silly. Men started to razz him about the burden he bore with us kids. He swiftly put a Stop to our behavior. He must have needed time with adults - poor man.

We often heard the remark "pobres huerfanas" (poor orphans). "Da me la Josephine or da me la Christela". (Give me Josephine or give me Christela). That terrified us. Adults should be more cognizant of the impact that their words and actions have on children. With their tongue several women would wet their fingertip and made the sign of the cross on our forehead. This was done in order to prevent them from giving us "Mal del Ojo" (the evil eye). The theory was, if someone stared admiringly at a child for too long a period the child would become ill, fussy, vomit, etc. One lady actually spat on my forehead and stuck a piece of blue paper from out of her tobacco pouch on my forehead as she made the sign of the cross. I avoided her like the plague after that.

I remember the old horse drawn wagon as Dad and I headed out to the mountains to chop wood used for heating our home and cooking meals. He harvested enough wood to last throughout the freezing winter. I thought my Father a tower of strength. The horses obeyed and did as he demanded.

Other trips to the Cibola forest were for securing posts and all the work was accomplished manually using an axe followed by loading the posts into the horse drawn wagon to transport them home. Once home he cut the posts to size and shaped them perfectly at either end. Next, he crisscrossed them in rows of ten until the stack contained 100. Our yard was visible from the highway and he posted a sign advertising them for sale. One day he was missing some stacks of posts and he had Candie drive him to the nearby villages in search of them. They finally were successful at a wood yard in Belen where he proved they were in fact his since he had marked them with tacks.

A staple for my Father when we went into the forest was Osha, an herb from the parsley family. The herb has a very pungent odor. We always carried a piece of the dry root in our pocket to deter snake attacks. It is used to treat wounds and sores and is believed that a piece of the dry root should be kept in your pocket to prevent a surgical wound from becoming infected. An old wife's tale claimed that some people tend to be infectious and the root is a safeguard. The dry root was also chewed to aid stomach disorders and headaches. Osha is one of the most useful herbs.

Prior to our mountain outings we packed a lunch of tortilla, water, beans, potatoes or other leftovers that were on hand. Other times we stopped at Don Luciano Padilla's Store and purchased potted meat, chips, soda, a Jack Horner Pie or a Big Hunk candy bar. These snacks were a big deal to me and I ate my lunch while playing underneath the wagon then took a long nap.

When inclement weather did not permit that I accompany Dad he left me in the care of Juanita Candelaria a teacher at Manzano Elementary. She was very kind and loving to me. I remember making ducks using wire to mold the body, next we covered them with layers of paper brushing on glue until they took shape. When they were set and dry, we painted the beaks orange and the body white. Next, we inserted little realistic eyes on their faces. The ducks had a hollow where one could store small items. I helped Mrs. Candelaria make copies for home and class assignments by working a hand cranked mimeograph machine. The machine forced a wine-colored ink through a stencil onto paper. The gelatin like substance was delicious!! (probably poisonous)

In 2007 by coincidence Juanita was our neighbor in S.E. Albuquerque. We became reacquainted as we belonged to the same parish and attended 11:00 a.m. Sunday Mass. We took her to museums, out to lunch and I walked over in the evening to visit her as my husband worked the evening shift. I assisted her with potting plants, sorting mail, and we never lacked for conversation. She enlightened me when she shared that she requested that Dad leave me in her care. Since she had no children of her own, her desire had been to adopt me however Dad refused to separate his family. All of those years I believed that I had been an imposition on her and the class and thought "what nerve of Dad to use her as a baby sitter while she was working".

The people in the village helped their family and neighbors in tragedy and through rough spells. It is my opinion that we are a product of our upbringing, culture, the people we are associated with, our social and economic status, and education. The modern term is "it takes a village to raise a child."

The Candelarias lived on a large ranch near Red Canyon and Fourth of July Campgrounds, and both of them were well educated. I was extremely impressed by the home with its sun porch and in-law casita. Juanita loved antiques and she blended them beautifully with all the other furniture. The home was spotless, inviting, and warm. Eleno's military career had taken him abroad and there were many collectables to admire.

I certainly didn't think of us as orphans to feel sorry for. I had so much love and attention. In addition, I had my playmate Christela and my niece Carmen Lou one year my junior who spent summers with us and we with them in Albuquerque. We had the run of the home and grounds in Manzano. By this time the home had electricity which was very minimal so we connected a long extension cord and ran it from the front end of the home through a door to a small room at the rear end of the house. We were able to force the cord through a small hole on the door which was sealed shut. This gave us power and allowed us to play our 45 and 78 speed records. We danced up a storm!! This smaller room was our private little home of 12 x 6 feet. We kept our toys and dolls, a small table and chairs on one end. The opposite end was our living area with a small cot. The room sat situated directly behind the large salon which had been Grandfather Eleno's store and had probably been used for storage of goods and as a receiving area in the 1800's. This room had, at one time, the only outside door leading to the West with a road and an irrigation ditch running behind it.

Manzano had heavy rain downpours in my childhood days. The arroyos ran with such great force that the force of the runoff displaced large boulders, outhouses, trash, driftwood, and destroyed roads or anything else that got in its path.   One of these storms caused the acequia (ditch) behind our home to rupture engulfing our home with water.   I remember many men from the community wearing boots and hauling buckets full of water attempting to keep the water from completely destroying our home. I was about 5 years old and there were men in uniform which scared me; I don't know what I thought; however, I recall hiding behind the fireplace in the room with the bay window.

One of the things Dad did after the flood was take to the arroyos for the purpose of hauling numerous loads of rocks and boulders in his squeaky horse drawn wagon. He then fitted together these rocks which were of various sizes comparable to building a stone wall, then filled the crevices with sand and continued stacking until they were the height of the windows; about four feet high. He layered rocks in this fashion all along the home wall the length of the home which is 50 feet and angled them at a 45-degree angle until they met our property line near the ditch bank. Finally, he sealed the whole thing with cement. He worked like a mad man wearing coveralls, a long shirt, a wide brimmed straw hat, and a handkerchief tied around his forehead to keep the perspiration away from his thick eye glasses. You would think he was racing to beat the next rain storm. He was a very hairy man similar to a bear. The front and rear of his shirt were soaked with perspiration as were his forehead and underarms. During that flood we lost the use of the West door and only used the top part as a window.

South of "our playroom" was another large room which was never restored or used after the flood. There was no flooring in that room and it smelled of dirt, therefore it was closed off. People in the old days were superstitious or maybe just story tellers with great imaginations. Whatever the case legend had it that Grandfather Eleno hid money and gold coins under the flooring in that room. It was said that at night one could see a bright ray of light emitting from the window which supposedly signified where a treasure was hidden. As per our Father the story goes that in digging for the monies an indentation was found in the ground revealing the shape of a large can. They concluded that the treasure had already been unearthed. I am not clear if the flooring was removed while searching for the hidden treasure or if it was lost during the flood.

The flood warped most of the flooring throughout the home, some worse than others. Eventually Dad placed sheets of plywood in our kitchen, small bedroom, and living room/bedroom, and fireplace room. They were covered with wall to wall linoleum. In addition, the fireplace became unstable and was repaired using bricks to stabilize the foundation and was given a brick face.

All these years later, 65 plus, a grant was obtained because the ditches remained unstable and now there is an underground system in place to enable farmers to irrigate there fields efficiently and safely.

Carmen Lou, Christela, and I took advantage of our freedom and got creative with our mud pies by helping ourselves to eggs from the chicken nests and added them to the mud because we thought the eggs would prevent our cakes from cracking??? or so we hoped. We played in the barns and climbed the rafters then jumped into the hay. We played dress-up with high heel shoes and prom dresses that had been left hanging in the closets by my older sisters.

Dad made a very tall swing for us, a merry-go-round, installed a tether ball pole gifted to us by our siblings, and made us zancos (stilts). My brother Eleno allowed Elena and James to stay several weeks during the summer. I was 11 or 12; they were 4 and 5 years old. I loved the companionship and playing Mommy to them. I was responsible for the cooking and got fancy by adding food coloring to the mashed potatoes. I will never live down the day they caught me pouring powdered milk into a fresh milk container. I felt forced to try to fool them because they would only drink fresh milk which was a luxury we seldom enjoyed. The three of us put on little concerts and we enacted marriage ceremonies – these were wonderful times.

We made new friends in grade school and were allowed to have play overs. My friends were Cecilia, Mary Lou, Stella, Rose Mary, and Lourdes. Christela had her own set of friends – Sally, Oralia, Diana, and Magdalena.

Manzano School

Sally came from a family of 16 children. Her older brother Delfin married my sister Candie. When Sally was little she lost an eye to a rock thrown by her brother Abelicio so she was fitted with a glass eye. Christela did not want me around at times and Sally called me a "big fat pig" so that I would leave them alone. In return I called her "Little blind chicken" "pew, pew, pew" and that made her run home in tears. At the time I guess I thought turnaround was fair play. What it really amounted to was a form of bullying on both our parts.

Our friend's parents served as second Mothers to us. Oralia 's Mom made outfits for my dolls and altered our clothing. They all were kind and generous to us. Mary also had 14 siblings and her Mom invited me to sit and share dinner. As an adult I was told that they often went without meals and even borrowed a cup of sugar here, a cup of flour there, an egg, etc; whatever it took to complete a dish. Their home always had music as her Father and several of her brothers played guitar and sang.   I thought it to be a very joyful place. Their situation reminded me of the life portrayed in the novel Angela's Ashes.

The memories I have about Mercedes, Sally's mom, are more about feelings than the spoken word. I recall what it felt like entering that large home through the back entrance. Once you made it up the stairs there was a little room where coats and firewood were kept. I looked for a reason to enter to the left which led to the kitchen. It usually didn't occur to Sally or Maggie to offer us the freshly baked goodies nor the food left on the stove warmer - That took some hinting on our part.

Sena (pronounced senia) Mercedes (a polite way to address your elders) routinely baked moyetes (sweet anise rolls with raisins), pastelitos (fruit pies), and biscochitos (anise cookies). The home smelled of fruit and was filled with wonderful aromas. As though she didn't have enough mouths to feed, Christela and I felt welcomed. In those days it was impolite to ask someone if they wanted to eat, have you eaten or are you hungry? Instead, you set a plate at the table and said "arrimate a comer" (sit here and eat).

Sena Mercedes was very resourceful and made "queso blanco" (white cheese) and quajada (yogurt) with milk from the cows. The Herrera children would hit the streets of Manzano on foot selling these items. What a feast when we could afford to purchase these delicacies. We sprinkled sugar or poured syrup over the queso savoring every last bite.

It is said that when the home they lived in initially came up for sale Sena Mercedes had enough saved up money from her business ventures to purchase it. Forward 40 years and seldom did you find Sena Mercedes, now living in Albuquerque with family, without her needle in hand. She crocheted table cloths and doilies by the hundreds which embellished the homes of all her children and grandchildren. She also crocheted long infant baptismal gowns with matching bonnets and laced them with blue or pink ribbons as appropriate for her Grandchildren.

In 1996 we lost our 25-year-old son Joseph to an automobile accident. Sena Mercedes now in her 80's was wheelchair bound, never-the-less she attended the funeral services. At the reception I approached her to thank her for attending and she cried. I hugged her and told her "don't cry he is not suffering"; she responded in her harsh trembling voice "I am not crying for Joseph; I am crying for you" **Wow!**

We visited with the Lopez family – they had Orlando, Cecilia, Ursula, Jose, Ricardo, and Alfonso. In addition, they had Antonio a bedridden invalid son who could not speak but made loud moaning sounds while lying in bed. I don't recall him ever being out of the bed. He was wounded at war and Mrs. Lopez attended to his every need for probably 40 years until she couldn't any longer, then Cecelia took over his care.

As was the custom in those days you offered coffee to your guests. Dona (pronounced Donia) Lola Lopez proudly asked one of her daughters to open a can of fruit to go along with the coffee. Fruita (fruit) in a store bought can was extravagant in those days and we knew she was proud to have it on hand. A child knows who loves them and returns the gesture. Our way of showing them how we felt was by elevating them to Tia (aunt) Lola and Tio Santiago. When Manzano was in need of a grade school they donated the property with the stipulation that it would revert to the family should the school be vacated. Many decades later the property was returned to the Lopez's and their son Ricardo converted the school house into a home for his large family.

Six years ago, I witnessed this gesture earned. Our son Paul and wife Mariana were fostering 3-year-old Ayla and 5-year-old Garrick. It was not long before Ayla called them Mommy and Daddy. Garrick was a little slower but he too began to address them as Mommy and Daddy and I know for a fact this was without prompting. It was a beautiful sight to witness.

My Father was able to read and write in Spanish but was not capable of helping us with our home work after the 2nd grade. He did ensure that we sat at the table and completed our homework assignments. Christela fell asleep trying to get through them many times.

He was a stickler about our attendance and behavior and was vigilant about it into high school. Periodically he stopped at the Administration Office in Mountainair wearing his infamous coveralls and high-top shoes to inquire about my older siblings and of course I went along.

When my sister Lala was a senior in high school at 17 Dad was informed that she had not reported to school on that particular day and neither had her boyfriend Albert. Lala was really in for a good belting and then some??. The school bus approached Manzano in the afternoons and dropped off the students on the right side of the street first, circled around further into town by the church then allowed the remaining students to exit. The little spy that I was, I ran to the first stop and told Lala about our findings earlier in the day. She decided not to exit the bus instead she returned to Mountainair where she spent the night.

She had worked at Johnson's Café in Mountainair and had hidden inside the hem of her room curtains several 20 dollar bills. She reported to work at 6 a.m. and I accompanied her one morning. I was amazed that she put on her make-up as she drove the thirteen mile stretch.   On occasion Dad, Christela, and I ate at the restaurant and ordered a hamburger, milk, and cherry pie ala mode. I thought it magic when she lifted the heavy stainless-steel spout and cold milk came gushing out. As I recall we left without paying, leaving her responsible for our bill.

The purpose of her working was to earn money for school clothes and other needs. Underneath her bed she had a case of hair spray and petty coats in different colors. She loved her make-up and sundries as well and she was gorgeous.

Back to the bus incident - Lala asked me to retrieve the money from her bedroom curtains and give to Cecilia so that she could have it the following morning. She chose not to face the wrath of Dad, but decided to board the train to Belen where our brother Eleno and sister Candie picked her up. She enrolled at Valley High School in Albuquerque and was allowed to return for graduation with her class in Mountainair.

That was an abrupt and extremely painful ending to our surrogate Mother. I was 9 years old and Christela was 13. The following days I wore a bandana at school and I refused to remove it because I did not have fresh braids. From that day forth we became in charge of household duties; what a rude awakening for us. We loved and missed her so much. She worked miracles with food; she was a master at baking breads and made natillas, empanadas, bisochitos, pastelitos, egg torta, sopa, jelly, and all the traditional foods. We ate fried chicken (from our coop), biscuits and gravy, fudge made with sugar and cocoa, caramelo, ice cream using snow, vanilla, and food coloring and syrup from caramelized sugar for our pancakes.

Again, fast forward to 1996 when we lost our son Joseph to an automobile accident. Now adults the Lopez families with spouses and several children were there for us. Cecilia and her husband Bobo belonged to our parish community and without our requesting them, they brought folding tables and chairs. People also brought armloads of food and drinks for the numerous friends, neighbors, and relatives attending this solemn occasion. Exactly how does one distinguish the difference between a true friend and a relative???

The Otero's from El Gato (The Cat) had an impact on my life. Their youngest son Albert was my age; he became ill during first grade and did not live long. This is the first time I can remember experiencing the loss of someone to death. Our young class was devastated.

Cruz Otero and my Father visited in the living room at the ranch while Christela and I stayed with Sena Leonor in the kitchen watching her prepare lunch. As she attended to the large pot of beans simmering on her wood burning stove, she made small talk and joked with us. She was about 5 feet tall, slightly overweight, and wore her hair tied back. She wore an apron and perhaps that is where I get my habit. Wearing an apron in the kitchen for me is comparable to my fastening my seat belt when I get into my automobile.

She made dough for tortillas and set it aside while she peeled and sliced potatoes. Once the potatoes were frying, she began to roll out the small fat tortillas with practiced perfection. First the tortilla was placed on the hotter area of the stove for a bit then turned over. When it was cooked, she moved that tortilla to the right edge of the stove to be kept warm and the pile grew taller. She continued tending to that stack by alternating the pile.

Next, she sliced ring bologna and added it to the fried potatoes – that got our mouth to watering. She wrapped the tortillas in a towel and set them on the center of the table along with a cube of butter. You could slip the tip of your finger in between the tortilla separating it and turn it into a little envelope to stuff with potatoes. She put small amounts of beans, potatoes, and chile in serving bowls and set them on the table as well. When the table was set with dishes and silverware, she had us invite the men in to eat. What a feast that was!!

It was expected by our Father that we help clear the table, wash, and dry the dishes. I now realize how much work and preparation it takes to have company over yet she seemed to do it with little effort.

As an adult Sena Leonor's advice to me and many others was "When you become a mother-in-law you see nothing and you hear nothing". Pretty smart lady.

In anticipation of these visits, Dad was prepared with a little something to gift; It might be two cans of store-bought fruit, or fresh produce. He called this "Granjear"(to impart). All us girls still follow the tradition of imparting a gift of labor when we bake, make a special dish, etc.

I could continue along this line as I have an abundance of vivid memories, however, I will tell you that each day ended with me sitting on Dad's bed removing the days accumulation of dirt between each toe using my fingers prior to reciting my prayers. I fell asleep with my head tucked into his armpit. He remarked that I was asleep before my head hit the pillow. All these years I thought that to be an exaggeration until a few years ago when I witnessed my Grandchildren doing the same. It is truly amazing.

While every generation becomes better educated, one might think that we would learn the "Mal" (bad) effects that bullying and corporal punishment have on an individual. During researching and contemplating on my past I could not help but observe these damaging behaviors continue. Today we are seeing child abuse, bullying, crime, discrimination, alcoholism, and sexual abuse. I am not blind to the negative behaviors I have witnessed in my life.

At home we spoke Spanish and I was taught English in elementary school. While I appreciate the value of mastering a new language, I feel it was done at great cost to our self-esteem. We were admonished for speaking Spanish and criticized for mispronouncing English words. It was a no-win situation. We were encouraged to use the English version of our names i.e. Maria/Mary; Juan/John; Magdalena/Maggie; Miguel/Mike; Consuelo/Connie and so on. Our sister Dulcinea has been called Candie to this day. Many of us still believe that the English version is superior (we drank the kool-aid). The premise of changing our names was for us to assimilate with the Anglo-Saxon culture. Once changed these names became permanent and were used on our report cards, our diplomas, employment records, driver's license, marriage certificates, utility bills and voter registration.

The English version of our names worked well until 2005 when Congress enacted the REAL ID Act which set standards for the issuance of sources of identification. The act dictates that an applicant must produce proof of residency, a birth certificate and Social Security information. These adopted names were no longer legitimate and proved to be problematic when it came to renewing a driver's license, voting and air travel. If you were in possession of a current passport you were in luck as it was accepted. However, I know of several people who paid over $100 to renew their passport so that they could continue to use the name which they had become accustomed to. As a result, the given name as shown on their birth certificate is reflected on their driver's license, but they still go by the English version. _How does that compute??_

In sixth grade we had a male teacher who snuck up behind female students when we had our elbows on the desk and he patted our breasts from behind. We were not mature enough to wear bras, however we were somewhat developed. I told my father about his behavior and my father was furious. That week-end my brother Eleno and my brother in law Fred drove from Albuquerque to meet with the principal. They demanded that the teacher cease touching me. When the school year ended that teacher did not promote me to seventh grade although all my grades were passing. Again, my brother spoke to the principal and I was promoted "on condition".

After 6th grade I would be bused to Mountainair Junior High School 13 miles from Manzano. As my siblings before me, I would need to help support myself. I spent that summer in Albuquerque with my sister Cecilia and her family. Cecilia secured employment for me cleaning houses in an affluent area twice a week.   Those jobs were a challenge for me as I was very shy, soft spoken, and insecure. I had never operated a dish washer, floor buffer, or an automatic washing machine. At home I washed clothing in our Maytag wringer type washing machine.

I did my very best and the ladies kept me on throughout the summer. One of the homes had two teenagers who swam, sun bathed and read books. We never conversed or became acquainted, and they told their friends that I was their maid. I did not appreciate being referred to by that term but kept it to myself. It was obvious to me that the dishes were left on the counter top all week awaiting my return and I recall perspiration running down my face as I scoured the caked-on food on the mountain of pots, pans, plates, and glasses prior to putting them in the dish washer.

Junior high school was a culture shock to us all. In the first place I was about 60 pounds overweight. My well-intentioned sister Cecilia grabbed at my large breast one day and tossed two bras at me saying "wear those, you look like a cow."   The bras in those days were not like the soft form fitted bras of today. They were stiff and padded with stitching that circled from the tip of the nipple to the inner part closer to the ribs.   I suppose they were made to enhance the breast size. I was already well endowed and now looked huge and did not need enhancing so I refused to wear them. I took to wearing a little black sweater over everything to hide my nipples and bouncing breasts. Eventually I came across two gently worn bras and now I begun to wear a bra. Purchasing sanitary napkins was another ordeal, but fortunately Dad did not comment when I put a box in the shopping cart. My sisters had enlightened me earlier as to what I should expect during menstrual cycles. It takes a tender, loving, and perceptive Mother to help an adolescent's transition through these periods and Dad fell short in that respect.

The classmates bused from Manzano had never been around Anglo students and we all spoke with a Spanish accent. We were made to feel that they were better than we were. Mrs. Johnson, our teacher had us take turns reading out loud and I felt self-conscious. The boy who sat at the desk in front of me was in much worse shape than I. He literally shook, and the desk moved when he was called upon to read. That caused more anxiety for me as I would be called upon next.

Junior high and high school were housed in the same campus, however they had separate buildings and we shared the same cafeteria and gymnasium. I was very modest and it was difficult when it came time to shower after PE class because with the open showers there was no privacy. The Anglo girls paraded around naked while we opened our locker doors to hide away a little while getting dressed. We had to become accustomed to change classrooms, teachers, and keep our books in lockers.

Eventually it all became routine and I did fairly well. During those two years I became interested in boys in particular a boy named Chris. Our eyes would meet as we passed in the hallways during breaks yet we were both too shy to communicate past "Hi".

My sister-in-law Gigi was very supportive of me. She made several outfits for me to camouflage my weight by adding oversized pockets and boxed pleats on the skirt.

One outfit had a matching vest that hung just below the waist line. The clothing helped to uplift me and improved my self-esteem.

My friend Lourdes rented a mail box at the Mountainair Post Office and I decided to do the same as I had a guy from Estancia that wanted to write me. I knew that Dad would tear up the letters as he had with my sister Lala. After a while Lourdes and I decided to share one box and share the expense in order to reduce our cost. Out of habit and curiosity I still peeked into my old box and found that the combination had not changed. Lourdes dared me to take an air-mail letter just out of curiosity – we were trembling after opening it when we discovered two $20.00 bills inside. A GI (solider) had sent the money to his family. While we thought to return the letter and money to the mail box, we felt the risk was too great. In our minds we envisioned our finger prints being traced and what a great crime we would be charged with. Subsequently Lourdes kept one twenty and I bought my Dad a Very Large Print Spanish Bible thinking this purchase would atone for my sin.

By the end of Junior High school, two years later, I was becoming more receptive to growth and new ideas and had made several new friends.
That summer Dad, Christela, and I took a bus trip to Juarez, Mexico. That was a vacation of our lives and for some reason it appeared to us to be very extravagant. Our Father was in his glory carrying conversations with the numerous people at the Plaza Park. He declared that the Mexican people were a joyful people as musicians roamed the park playing their instruments and singing requested songs for tips. The Cathedral of Guadalupe sat across the street from the park and all the Masses were filled to capacity with organ music and loud singing spilling out into the streets. Once exiting Mass, Mexican vendors approached you selling their wares. This was an excellent opportunity to bargain. Food prepared at resident's homes were sold by families. There were many

handicapped individuals begging for money outside the church steps which saddened us and made us feel uncomfortable. During our short stay in Juarez, Christela and I had our hair styled for probably the second time in our lives. My hair was styled with ringlets at the top of my head and the balance of my hair remained down and curled. You might see this hair fashion on the bride at her wedding, even beautiful by today's standards. Christela's short cut was equally nice.

Next, we had colored 8 x 10 portraits taken and they were centered on an oversized matt ready to be framed in glass. Our complexion in these portraits was enhanced by adding lip gloss, blush on our cheeks, and our eyebrows were given more emphasis. In addition, a reddish tone was added to my hair color and my eyes looked hazel. They made us resemble porcelain dolls.

La Dies y Seis de Septiembre (16th of September Ave.) was the main avenue in Juarez and there was a 5-Star restaurant called La Nueva Poblana. We were to meet Dad there at a given time. When we arrived, the waiter escorted us to our seat to accompany Dad. Christela and I could not stop ourselves from giggling because Daddy had lip stick around his lips. He had a twinkle in his baby blue eyes and I think he was a little tipsy therefore when we told him about the lipstick, he did not believe us. At that point the waiter wearing a white server's jacket with a towel over his forearm said to Dad "It is a fact" and handed Dad the towel so that Dad could wipe his face. The meal was 3-5 courses, 5-Star and I will not describe it in detail. It was beyond anything we had experienced previously.

We spent a lot of time at the multi-level Mercado (market) and Daddy decided to have his shoes polished and allowed me to do the same. At one point the shoe shine man had me remove my shoes to enable him to clean and polish my shoestrings. We tipped the shoeshine man, he accepted the tip, kissed the tip of his fingers gesturing a thank you and made the sign of the cross as he looked upward toward a mural of Our Lady of Guadalupe on the upper floor of the Mercado wall and we walked away. Several seconds later I recalled having a $20.00 bill inside my shoe; needless to say, it was gone. I ran back to find the man and he was long gone.

We purchased several souvenirs to gift our sisters and they were wrapped in newspaper and stored in the bottom compartment of the large bus during our trip home, many of them were made of clay and we found them broken into hundreds of pieces when we unpacked them upon reaching Albuquerque. Win some, lose some???

I also saw an optometrist and placed an order for contact lenses. In those days my glasses were comparable to coke bottle bottoms as I inherited my Dad's eye sight. The hard lenses arrived two weeks later and they were amazing and life changing, providing a great boost to my self-esteem; I wore them successfully throughout high school.

11 Mountainair Mustangs
High School

The summer prior to entering high school I seriously concentrated on shedding those excess pounds. At home we prepared our meals using lard. As I began to lose pounds, I envisioned my weight loss to a 5 pound can of lard. I lost 1, 2, 3, 4 and 5 Bingo!!!!

It bothered me that my best friend could not eat with me in the school cafeteria. Mary came from a family of 15 children and they simply could not afford $1.25 per week. I came up with a solution – every Monday we went to Tabet's Grocery Store where I purchased 10 slices of bologna and one loaf of bread, I had the butcher keep these items for us in his cooler. That left me enough to purchase one soda and one bag of chips per day which we shared to complete our meal.

The school cafeteria was offering two free meals for students who would work during lunch cleaning up the space and washing the stainless-steel food trays, pots, pans, etc. Mary and I bid for two of the positions; that provided lunch for her and one brother. I did not tell Dad I was earning my food therefore he continued to give me $1.25 per week. I ate free and sold my other 25 cent lunch to a classmate. Now I had $1.25 per week to do with as I pleased.

My brother Eleno, now in sales, won a transistor radio which he gifted me and we absolutely enjoyed the heck out of it and felt very worldly walking down the street listening to it. I was the first person to own a bike also a gift from my sisters.

Our older siblings visited Manzano on week-ends to see how we were faring and brought ingredients for preparing meals such as meat loaf, round steak with gravy and other special meals. They took us to wedding, shower, and fiesta dances in Torreon at La Sala de Fidel (dance hall and bar) owned by Mr. Garcia. We made the rounds of dances in the nearby communities. In the hall there were benches all along the perimeter where married couples sat. It was not unusual to bring an infant and lay it on a blanket underneath the bench. I don't recall toddlers or young children at these dances. I have been told that women brought infants because they needed to nurse them. These dances were open to the public and people from surrounding communities attended.

The unattached girls stood at the rear of the hall and the boys tapped them on the shoulder requesting a dance. If the dance went well the couples stood visiting in the center of the hall until the band played the next song. I was not good at flirting or idle conversation and therefore was not asked to dance as often. It was said of me "Se cree muy suave" (she thinks she is too good). In reality I was extremely shy. My sisters and sister-in-law brought me some of their dresses to wear. I loved a black and white suit that Candie let me wear with its' long jacket and pencil skirt. Another favorite was a grey wool skirt with matching vest. The vest was trimmed in a gold suede and it had a long sleeve matching gold crepe blouse. By this time, she worked for the telephone company, had no children and bought herself nice clothing, that worked well for me. Christela, four years my senior had a figure to die for and she looked lovely in everything she wore. She had much prettier clothing than I because she worked summers.

One tradition at wedding dances was La Marcha (wedding march) where one couple led and all other couples followed. Skillful leaders were in high demand. The formations could become quite intricate and varied. At times couples separate, at one point the head couple stood about two feet apart facing each other, raised their arms and laced their fingers together to form an arch. As couples pass through the arch, they also raise arms and become part of the existing arch and it becomes longer. It is great fun with a lot of joking, laughing, visiting, and carrying on. The head couple is responsible for all couples to end up with the same partner after every separation otherwise the march became one big chaotic mess. The march ends with the bride and groom in the center of the dance floor with everyone else forming several circles around them representing a large layered wedding cake. The march music stops, a slow song is played and the wedded couple dances by themselves. Meanwhile the guest dancers line up to dance with the newlyweds. They form two single files, the women behind the Padrino (best man) and the men behind the Madrina (maid of honor) to take a turn at the dollar dance. You gave the money to the Madrina or Padrino for the privilege of a dance. Monies collected were used to fund the honeymoon or provide for other necessities. Children were allowed at wedding dances and they always had a great time.

Another tradition during the dance was the Entriega de novios (surrender of the newlyweds) Someone was commissioned to sing a very long Copla (song/verses) consisting of both fixed and improvised verses which congratulate, admonish, and bless the newlyweds and their families in their new set of relations.

We became acquainted with other young people from the surrounding communities and many courtships lead to marriage. Several cases, as I recall led to 2 sisters marrying 2 brothers. Reason being that one brother accompanied the other and met the younger sibling.

At times a fight broke out during the dance mainly having to do with rivalry or a jealous boyfriend. The females leaped onto the stage where the band played to afford them a safe place. The fight didn't last long and the young boys only used their fists.

There were several successful bands that came from those mountain communities. Sidros' Armada performed in Las Vegas, Nevada for over a decade and won many awards. Initially the band consisted of the family members with the Father Agapito an excellent accordion player. When "The Garcias" played in Willard, their hometown, people from villages throughout Torrance County attended. You were sure to have a packed house. Today Sidro plays the saxophone around Albuquerque with Freddie Chavez.

Los Garrapatas originated in Torreon and they are still performing and they have produced several popular CD's featuring favorite New Mexican music. Learning and practicing an instrument was a favorite pastime in those days and it was also a family tradition.

La musica has been an essential part of everyday life from the cradle to the grave; it leavens and sweetens our most private and public rituals. With our songs we find inspiration and are transformed. The passions of the spirit are revealed and shared.

Our Father prohibited us from dating therefore we had to meet our boyfriends in secret if we wanted to pursue a relationship. After a dance a young man insisted on walking me to my car and we met up with Dad waiting for me. He asked the young man to leave and my friend made a disrespectful remark to Dad. We drove home in silence, parked the vehicle in the garage and Dad spoke candidly to me. I realized he was crying when he said "you don't understand the predicament you put us both in". Somehow, he did reach me and I truly felt sorry for him.

I loved my high school chorus class and received the Chorus Award one year. I participated in 2 operettas and still remember the songs. At one operetta I played the comedy role of an old spinster and all these years later I sang and acted it out for my three Granddaughters

Arianna, Raquel, and Esperanza and they take turns imitating me. They love putting on my apron, a turban, oversized shoes and pretend to sweep the floor with a broom in hand, they open the oven door and we have great fun!   The song ends with the lyrics "and smile to please though I am dead, I'd rather be aaaa-spinster" tossing the broom they drop to the floor. As children do they say "let's do it again Grandma," "let's do it again!!"

Mrs. Sloan the chorus teacher lived directly behind the school building and took the class to her home for refreshments. She served us snacks in her fine china which made us feel special. That was my first experience with anything of that sort.

My friend Lourdes and I traded clothing which made us feel as though we had a new wardrobe for the week – that was fun! She was the first person I knew to live in a blended family and the first person to live in a prefabricated home. I thought them to be wealthy.

My home economics teacher Mrs. Argo taught us a whole lot about etiquette, table setting, posture, proper diet, sewing, packing, gift wrapping, etc. She invited me to travel to Wyoming to visit her family. True to form Dad said no. I was a cheerleader my junior and senior year and loved everything about the experience especially out of town trips. We were allowed certain items from the menu and I learned what chicken fried steak was for the first time. Us girls sang all the way and fell asleep in one another's arms on the way home after a late night.

I attended two proms the first one of which ended abruptly and very early. I really think Dad must have known something was up when he allowed me to spend the night at Andrea's home that Saturday. I invited Jack from Torreon whom I had danced with and thought I loved. He picked me up at Andrea's and I was so proud to be seen dancing with him. Before long he wanted to go out to the car and rather than appear to be "a stick in the mud" I consented. His intentions were not honorable and he justified himself by telling me that we could marry if I got pregnant. When I continued to refuse, he warned that he would take me home and "Damn him" he took me back to Andrea's. My magical prom night ended very early.

My Senior year I was football queen and class vice-president. We voted to collect glass bottles as a fund raiser to enable us to pay bus transportation for a senior class trip to Colorado. My Dad dropped me off many times as he drove the car slowly while I collected several trunk-loads of bottles. That trip was the first time that I sat next to or communicated with an Anglo-Saxon boy and found that he was extremely kind. I fell asleep with my head on his shoulder. It helped me to let go of my stereotypical perceptions.

I realize that my perception of things caused me to miss out on numerous opportunities. While attending class reunions many years later, now mature and open to other nationalities I and old classmates have had meaningful conversations. They too had many misperceptions about us and we find that we were all in the same boat with our insecurities. Many of these girls came from large, hard-working, poor ranch families and they also had to deal with difficulties in adapting.

The previous pages relate the story of my ancestors dating to the early 1800's. As I was contemplating on where I am today, I felt compelled to
delve into my past to see if I could make sense of it all.

When I was made aware of how my father was raised by a father who ruled with an iron fist during his impressionable years, it became clearer to me why our family was raised with a strict discipline which left no room for discussion or negotiation. He was left a widower at 50 years old responsible for 7 children. For him it was a life changing event emotionally, physically, and financially. Up to that time mother had been his co-parent allowing him the freedom to provide for his family wherever employment opportunities led him. He worked for the railroad and the WPA etc. and would be gone several months at a time. With his wife's death he could ill afford to leave his young family unattended. His employment opportunities narrowed and his legal blindness was an additional obstacle. He was angry, broken hearted, devastated and probably afraid. It is no wonder that he reverted back to a parenting style resembling his own father's. He was unwavering in his tough, harsh, and uncompromising discipline and he expected a lot of support from the older children. They too were broken hearted, angry devastated and afraid, but in addition they were expected to become instant adults and at least partially self-supporting. He commanded respect and ruled with fear mixed with a good dose of love. Dad creatively carved out a living by farming, ranching, harvesting wood, lumber. and any other efforts that would keep him close to home all while keeping a very close eye on his family. There was very little mischief that we could get into without his being aware.

I was left without a mother at 3, but was showered with love and attention from everyone. I am thinking that dad got some consolation from me since it was difficult for many men in those days to embrace their older children or exhibit affection. He was also very stingy with praise.

Christela at 7 was a bed wetter until it was surgically corrected and was admonished for this daily. She must have suffered a great many emotions yet she was too young to understand what she was facing. Among my memories of Christela was of a Saturday night as my sister was bathing and a stranger stormed through the front door. He was driving to Punta de Agua and observed fire billowing from a dormer window. It wasn't long before several other neighbors and passersby got to work drawing water from the well extinguishing the fire with minimal damage to the inside. My sister was traumatized by this incident and continued to experience problems with her GI tract. Daddy finally took her to a Curandera (healer) who diagnosed her as being "sospendida" or suspension resulting in the large colon being pulled out of place. This can be as a result of a shock to the system ending in physical or mental injury. The curandera uses a finger to manipulate the colon through the rectum to relieve the suspension. My sister was healed apparently by the actions of the curandera. She eventually graduated high school, married and had a son Peter. She was really never whole again and much of her adult life was spent battling emotional and psychological problems.

Candie at 15 had been mom's pet and confidant, perhaps because she was left without her twin. She was in her prime, full of life and a high school cheerleader. Now she was a surrogate mother in addition to working summers to help support herself. This load became too taxing for her and when my older sister Cecilia secured gainful employment for her in Albuquerque she jumped at the chance, took the job, and left the family home prior to graduating.

Lala, motherless at 13 really had no options and continued to take on the role as our mother until she left abruptly at the age of 17 as you have read earlier.

Prior to mom's passing in 1952, Frances, my oldest sister at 22 was married and living in Albuquerque with her husband and a toddler Carmen Lou. A short time prior to moms passing she had been involved in a car accident which left her in a coma for 3 months. She was left with a speech defect, lack of the sense of smell, and other physical disabilities. She was very proud and refused to take charity, but worked at the cafeteria at the University of New Mexico for many years followed by a career at Goodwill Industries from which she retired. She was left husbandless and handicapped, but this didn't stop her from living a full and independent life.

Cecelia, 21, and Eleno, 19 now mature adults were living in Albuquerque as well and were left to pick up the pieces while mourning mother's death. They were taking care of Frances, driving to Manzano on weekends to check on us and dad all the while maintaining some sense of normalcy with their own obligations and social lives.

The point I am making is yes my life was great, but I must give credit where credit is due. My father deserves much praise for his influence in my life, but also my siblings and my community lifted me up and embraced me making me feel secure. Due to my innocence I was shielded from the ill effects of growing up a poor orphan "Pobre Huerfana".

Cecilia, Josephine, Frances, Eleno and Candie 2013

Back Row – Eleno, Cecilia, Christela, and Santiago
Front Row – Candie, Lala, Josephine, and Frances
January 1977

I have been told that Mother's last instruction to her children was "take care of each other" – clearly that was taken to heart.

13 The Beloved Mother
Carmen

Maria Carmelita (Carmen) Morales Zamora was born on May 11, 1911 to Celestino Morales (BD1878) from Tome, N.M. Her Mother was Maria Silva (BD 1884) from Manzano, N.M.

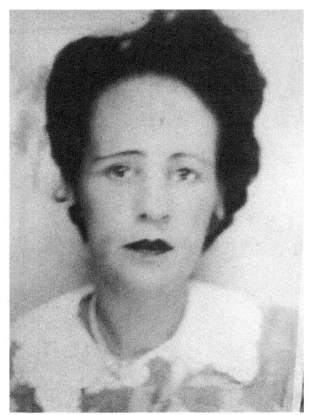

My Beloved Mother

She gave birth to ten children; Frances, Maria Cecilia, Valeria, Eleno, Dulcinea, Vicenta (twin to Dulcinea), Eulalia, Christela, Arturo, and myself Josephine. Birth dates at chapter end.

Mom died at the age of 41 on February 07, 1952 when I was three years old and although I don't remember her, I feel her presence to this day as she continues to be in the mind, heart, and lips of my siblings. First and foremost was her love for life, her family, and most of all her children. She loved to tell jokes, converse, and dance. Apparently, she was a very good-looking woman who took pride in how she dressed and groomed herself. As per my sister Candie her hair ringlets had to be perfect prior to going dancing. Candie was the only one allowed to style her hair in that fashion because Candie was able to hide the bobby pins.

Years after her passing I recall Dad and I watching our black and white television. Dad, due to his poor eye sight, laid on the floor on a rug while watching The Ed Sullivan Show one Sunday evening. Petula Clark came on and was wearing a dress that reminded him of one he bought for her. He cried and told me about that purchase and various others. He said "I never loved any other woman"

While we grew up poor as did most other families, Eleno, the only boy said that Mother always tried to please them. He recalled complaining that there was no dessert. Wouldn't you know she whipped up masa (dough) and made sweet sopapillas then sifted white powdered sugar on top especially for him.

I am told that she was a great homemaker. One year she painted the kitchen cabinets. The paint color was "Apple Green" this became a long-standing family joke. Mom swore the kids to secrecy, and they were not to reveal the paint color. She did not want other women to copy her color. She made curtains for all the rooms. To hold the family over for the winter she canned jars of jam from ours and neighbor's fruit trees.

Mom and my siblings also picked capulin (choke cherries) to make jam. One can't help but eat the cherries while picking and they are so potent but leave your tongue feeling thick plus they also leave a permanent stain on your clothing. Cascara de capulin, the bark of the bush was used for dyeing fabric and produced a beautiful red color.

They claim she was a great baker and made molletes (sweet rolls). Her hands were so accustomed to baking that she didn't have to measure out the ingredients. She broke open the eggs, beat them thoroughly, added a couple handfuls of sugar, anise seed, flour, and used her hand to scoop lard from a metal can. Next, she kneaded the dough to the perfect texture. She portioned out the rolls and made a shallow cross with a sharp knife in the center to form a cross reciting Jesus y Cruz (Jesus and this Cross). This resulted in perfect golden molletes every time. The most common form of bread was homemade tortillas usually made fresh daily. She baked bischotitos (anise cookies). This dough does not require yeast. You roll out the dough about ¼ inch thick similar to a tortilla but larger than a pizza. With a table knife you cut all shapes of pieces approximately 3 x 3 inches. Here the artistry begins – you cut small slits – about ¼ inch apart and roll the dough up any which way. It reminds me of baby fingers. There were many different designs that she formed. Next you dunk each cookie in a pre-prepared mixture of sugar and cinnamon then bake.

I won't describe the many foods of the day however some favorites were: sopa, sweet rice, papas con caldito, fidellos, and carne adovada. If you can imagine all this cooking and baking for a large family was done on a wood burning stove and water was brought in from the well outside.

Her sewing skills were polished as well. When blankets were frayed and old looking, she recovered them with beautiful patterns of cotton fabric. I grew up covered in these heavy blankets. Making a bed was an art all its own and beds were not to be sat on. They were for show and for sleeping. When making a bed these heavy blankets were tucked under at both sides prior to laying a chenille bedspread over them. It is no wonder she protected her beds so much – the mattresses in those days were of cotton and enclosed in Indiana (ticking). The inside of the ticking had several sets of straps so that the cotton could be evenly distributed. Once a year or so the cotton was emptied out, washed, placed on a large tarp and fluffed by using two long whips. She knelt with a whip on each hand and whipped the clean cotton to a nice fluff. Next, she re-stuffed the liner. In addition, she is remembered to have been a good seamstress. She made and mended clothing including cheerleading outfits - all with her foot pumped sewing machine.

The tin ceilings which had various patterns she painted using oil base paint and a paint brush. I have painted a ceiling or two that way and found it to be extremely difficult. For refreshing the abode wall, she made Calcimine (a white powdered suspension). Because of the oil lamps and the wood burning stoves used for cooking and heating the interior walls accumulated smoke.

Her life was filled with much joy as she had friends that she visited with, talked, walked, and played cards with. Candie could not understand what was so funny in the jokes she and her friends told while smoking a hand rolled cigarette.

I have experienced the death of a son and feel if an individual can live through that, everything else pales in comparison. Mom lost three children.
Dad doesn't remember details of how Valeria passed at two nor Vicenta at seven months. The passing of Arthur was in his memory as Mother was hospitalized in Albuquerque at the time. She was having various, as he put it, "female problems". They left Arthur in the care of Juanita Lopez and during that time Roman Garcia, a

cousin, received a call asking him to inform my parents that the infant was ill and was being driven to the doctor in Mountainair. Dad asked his brother in law Manuel Morales to take Mom home the following day and he took the train to Belen waited for another train that went South?? and he finally arrived in Mountainair at sunrise then hitched a ride to Manzano.

After being seen by the doctor, Cecilia my sister was sitting in the back seat of the car holding Arthur and she did not realize that the infant had died in her arms until they arrived at home and the women placed coins on the infants eye lids to keep them closed.

Mom continued to have health problems and passed the following year.

Children of Carmen and Santiago:
Frances	03-06-1930
Maria Cecilia	07-10-1931
Valeria	11-26-1932 – 11-21-1934
Eleno	02-02-1934 – 07-06-2018
Dulcinea (Candie)	02-08-1937
Vicenta	01-08-1937 – 08-02-1937
Eulalia (Lala)	04-09-1939 – 10-02-1989
Christela	06-24-1944 – 02-17-2110
Arturo	02-27-1951 – 1951
Josephine	04-08-1948

14 Father, Mother, Companion and Confidant
Santiago Zamora

My Father Santiago Zamora was born July 25, 1902 to Eleno and Vicenta. He had 13 siblings 4 of which were half siblings. (Detailed under Grandfather Eleno Zamora 1845).

My Father – Santiago Zamora

My Father grew up in Manzano, New Mexico and was an avid and animated story teller, a lost art these days. His stories and his clear memory continued to the end of his life at age 94. He possessed the ability to recall dates, times, places, and incidents. He knew people's names, extended relatives, and how much he earned and the year. In addition, he kept notes on a ledger which I now own. He marked his books with Black electrical tape so that he could easily refer to passages on the Bible, in novels, or on self-help medical books.

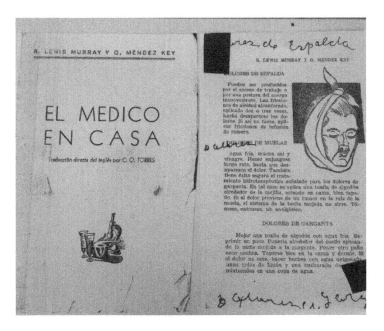

Medical Book

Osha, wild mountain parsley, was a staple. When going out into the fields you took a piece in your pocket. The pungent odor kept poisonous snakes away. It is also used to cure cold/flu by grating it and adding to diluted whiskey and drinking it. Other favorites were Canutillo for rheumatism; Alcanfor for headaches or dizziness; Aceite de Lampara 2 drops with a teaspoon of sugar for sore throat, cough, and chest pains; Cana Agria for sore gums or mouth; Canela for fainting or nausea; Hediondillo prevent and cure cancer; Mastranzo for stomach and respiratory ailments and numerous others.

One might think that Dad's type of memory is a gift when in fact it is a double edge sword. He carried too much hurt and excess baggage in the form of memories. He remembered who wronged him, who lied to him, who hurt him, etc. These hang-ups kept him from moving on after Mother passed and possibly from re-marrying, and having a joyous life. He claimed he would not remarry because he did not want to place estorvos (obstacles) in his children's paths. He felt that a step-mother would mistreat his children. Don't get me wrong; he had many interests and friends. He loved dancing, reading, visiting, repairing shoes using a vintage cast iron cobbler, carpentry, and seeing family but never a true confidant.

Cast Iron Cobbler

In 1971, a widower for 19 years, he left Manzano and relocated to Albuquerque.   I was living in Alaska at the time and regret that the home did not remain within the family. It is my opinion that the move helped him release much of the baggage he carried. He purchased a small bungalow dating back to the early 1900's on 8th Street near Mountain Road and walked to the grocery store, church, and frequented the park at Old Town and Well's Park where he met up with people his age and enjoyed having meaningful conversations, the thing he cherished most. He attended dances at Senior Centers and dated for the first time since Mothers death.

He took the city bus and visited his sisters Mercedes and Ramona. He hated that people took to reading books or newspapers on the bus for that was a lost opportunity for conversation. Tia Mercedes Lucero, one of his beloved sisters, treated him as though he were royalty – they talked for hours. The bus route passed the home where I lived in those days and I was his pit stop either over or back. He enjoyed that I cooked for him and my husband Jose Manuel (J.M) offered him a beer or a shot of hard liquor. He would respond to J.M.'s offer "Well, give me both".   Likewise, when I offered pancakes or eggs and he would replay "Well, give me both". Once fed he took a nap prior boarding the bus for home. He loved to eat and was not lazy about cooking for himself. He attempted eating at the senior citizen center but felt it was not enough food and cooked again upon returning home therefore he stopped eating at the senior center.

We all have memories of finding him preparing meals in a smoke-filled kitchen; because of his blindness he didn't see the smoke. He was happy making his sopapilla feast with the radio tuned to the Spanish station. He rolled out his dough in small rounds similar to a tortilla but with a small hole in the center. In order to keep up with the frying once the oil was hot these sopapillas were spread out all over the table and counter tops. Everything prepared he was ready to fry away without delays. They were damn good too!! He fried his eggs until the edges were crisp and absorbed the oil. Once he asked me to clean a large spot on the kitchen tiled floor; I thought he had vomited as it was yellowish. I kept gagging until he informed me that I was too particular and the spill was pumpkin.

My husband Jose and I have owned this historic bungalow located off Mountain Road near Old Town since 1996. One tenant who never knew Dad said she saw his ghost in the porch he converted to his bed room. She described him perfectly.

Many of the following tales are based on a tape-recorded interview done by Carmen Lou Padilla the oldest Grandchild (06-19-50 – 05-16-12) named after her 2 Grandmothers and the daughter of Pete and Frances Padilla, my oldest sister. Dad loved Carmen's visits as she was the only grand-daughter who spoke Spanish and sincerely was interested in what he had to say. Other tales are from my memory as he was my Father and Mother after the death of my Mother Carmen when I was 3 years old. My sisters Frances Padilla, Cecilia Bachicha, and Candie Herrera had input as did our brother Eleno Zamora prior to his death July 06, 2018.

Daddy (Santiago) felt that his youth was rich in that it was filled with many friends including his siblings namely; Ignacio, Casimiro, and Antonio. Specifically, he named 3 male sons of Juan Sanchez. They played at each other's homes and went into the forest to have picnics. They took cans of fruit, candy, meats and other items which they snuck from the family store. While in the forest they climbed trees and hung from them. On these outings they searched for eggs from Gavilanes (hawks).

Dad recalled a beating he got from his Father Eleno when he was given the job of transferring a herd of cattle from one field to another. Again, due to his poor eyesight, he lost a cow and he was not able to relocate it. His Father Eleno was not one for excuses. Earlier I told the story about a grade school incident where Dad received punishment and his nose were placed on the chalk board - this is a continuation of a school story. The Teacher Cecilio Quintana took to whipping the children with a long piece of board/wood on their hands – and he whipped his own son and extra 4 times because he was his son "Dad laughed about that". The young girls were not excluded either, he stated.

The teachers in those times did not have formal education and were more like baby sitters. Much of what they taught was repetition of phrases. They taught little songs ie; "Twinkle, twinkle, little star" and other short rhymes. There was not much to hold their interest therefore they played pranks on the girls by having them turn their heads and poking them with a sharp pencil on the cheek. They also pulled on their long-braided hair "There was no respect" he laughs; they shut the drawers on the girl's hands and put cuetes (firecrackers) in the wood burning stove.

The majority of the students were not interested in getting educated, however, there were exceptions. His brother Casimiro and Alejandro Sanchez were smart and studied. Casimiro stayed up until midnight studying and finally Grandfather Eleno agreed to allow him to attend school in Santa Fe but gave him zero financial support. After about 1 month, Casimiro was ready to return home for 2 reasons. One he was severely bullied and secondly, he felt he would starve. The school lunches in Santa Fe were served family style and by the time the platter got to Casimiro it was empty.

Dad did not dance growing up nor did he date. His first dance was at age 20 -21 with his 1st cousin Ramona Garcia at a wedding. We asked "how did you dress for dances?" and he replied "Mama Vicenta made us new shirts using the fabric from empty flour sacks, she also made our underwear". He recalls getting ready for a dance; his brother Ignacio was also getting ready and his Father Eleno had recently purchased new hats to sell at the store. Dad thinks his Father wanted Ignacio to be a model and show off the hats. These hats had pins, some with little bears, others with elephants. Ignacio simply refused to leave the home wearing one. His Father almost beat Ignacio to death but Ignacio would not give in. Dad felt that the children in those days were not treated with affection and were never praised. They were expected to work hard and carry their weight around the home, store, caring for the animals, and maintain the farm. In addition, they were to care for their parents.

"Times were hard for everyone", he stated. Women and children were to obey the head of the family. Wives were expected to be submissive to their husbands. His father felt that women had no place in business nor should they be present and partake in conversations with men. He recalls Grandfather Eleno telling Grandma Vicenta in that harsh loud voice "Oooh get out of here" – and she did.

In those times it was of utmost importance to baptize infants as soon as possible. Often times it was done the day after the infant was born. Another tradition regarding baptizing was: The Godparents, by themselves took the infant to be baptized at the church and then presented the child with the name "they" chose to the parents. When the child became an adolescent and completed catechism classes the parents asked a different Madrina or Padrino, depending on the sex of the child to confirm that child. Therefore, Catholic children have a couple who baptized them and one person who confirmed them. The confirmation Madrina or Padrino gave the child a middle name. The Catholic faith teaches that the Godparents who baptized the infant are responsible for stepping up should the parents not be able to bring up the child. My dad took great pains to document these names and dates on a ledger which he maintained.

Dad stated "Yo he passado los incomparables" (I have suffered the incomparable). The 1ˢᵗ automobile I owned was a Model T Ford which I obtained from a person in Estancia, NM. I traded for 1 ton of alfalfa. Because his impaired vision he could not obtain a driver's license, never-the-less, he drove about 30 years.

In those days it was common to hitchhike. There was a man "M. Lopez" who always wanted a free ride to Mountainair 13 miles away. "He never offered to pay a cent". One day I failed to pick him up. I parked in front of Tabet's Grocery Store and a State Police Officer came inside the store looking for me. He requested to see my driver's license. It was Dad's perception that Mr. Lopez reported him??? The Officer took Dad to the jailhouse. Dad spoke to Tomas Peralta, a gas station owner and respected community resident who requested a meeting before a Judge. He was fined $100.00 and his automobile was taken. (The fine was reduced to $30.00). "I had $25.00 on me and Tomas loaned me $5.00".

Shortly afterwards Dad sought assistance from a politician, Mr. Baca. He had someone drive him to Socorro, NM and was given a driving test and was awarded a driver's license.

After that, driving never set well with him and he made a surprise visit to Mr. Caster who was the Superintendent of Mountainair Schools. He pleaded that I be allowed to enroll in driver's education class. I became his Chauffer from that day on.

"I recall my posts getting stolen": He ventured out to the forest and cut posts to sell. These he crisscrossed in 10 until the stack contained 100. Our property was visible from the highway and he advertised them for sale. One day someone stole his posts. He had Candy, his daughter drive him around and finally located his posts in Belen. He recognized them because he had marked with them tacks, he did get them back.

As an adult, Dad worked for the railroad, worked the fields, tended to the farm animals, the fruit trees, vegetable garden, sold mountain size piles of pumpkins, harvested fire wood and vigas (fence posts) to sell and was employed by the WPA. In the later years he received Welfare.

Santiago (Dad) married Carmen when he was 29 years old and she was 20 or 21. He recalls her being a neighbor who lived about one city block from him. She was the love of his life and somehow (he couldn't say how) he knew that she was interested in him, therefore, he sent his mother Vicenta and her brother ??? to ask for her hand in marriage. They took with them a trunk full of "can't remember things". They married in the church in Manzano in 1929.

Old Church

Below is information taken from Dads ledger which is evidence of the importance Padrinos played in a child's life. They became the spiritual parents of the child, besides assuming full responsibility in the case of the death of the parents. They were chosen with the greatest of care. Affluent and well-beloved couples had up to a dozen plus god-children. Once a god- parent you became Compadres (Co-parent) to the children.

Together they had 10 children.

Following taken from Dad's ledger:

Child	Born	Died	God Parents
Frances	3/6/1930		Celestino and Socarrito Morales
Maria Cecilia	7/10/1931		Boleslo and Carolina Sanchez
Valaria	11/26/1932	11/21/1934	Antonio and Julianita Candelaria
Eleno	2/2/1934	7/6/2018	Santos and Carmelita Silva
Dulcinea	1/8/1937		Pedro and Abelina Mirabal
Vicenta	1/8/1937	8/2/1937	Juan and Lourdes Sanchez
Eulalia	4/9/1939	10/2/1989	Santiago and Isabela Silva
Arturo	2/27/1943	? /?/51	Tomas and Mercedes Lucero
Christela	6/24/1944	2/17/2010	Mateo and Premetiba Martinez
Josephine	4/8/1948		Manuel and Trinidad Morales

Francisquita Zamora nasio
El dia 6 de marzo en el año de
1930 sus padrinos son de Bautismo
Selestino morales y Socorrito morales

maria Cisilia Zamora nasio el dia
10 de Julio en el año de 1931 sus
padrinos son Bolais Sanchez y
Carolina Sanchez

Baleria Zamora nasio el dia 26
De Nabienbil en el año de 1932
Sus padrinos son antonio candelaria
y Jubanita candelaria

Eleno Zamora nasio el dia 2 de
Febrero en el año de 1934 sus
padrinos son Santos Silba y
Carmelita Silba

Dulsinea Zamora nasio el dia
8 de Enero en el año de 1937
Sus padrinos son Pedro mirabal
y abelina mirabal

Pirentta Zamora nasio el dia
8 de Enero en el año de 1937
Sus padrinos son Jose Sanches y
Siomires Sanches

Eulalia Zamora nasio el dia
9 de abril en el año de 1939
sus padrinos son Santiago Silva
y Isabella Silva

Ledger Book Page Showing Birthdates (1)

8

Cirtela Zamora nasio el dia
24 de Junio en el año de 1945
Sus padrinos son mateo martines
y premitiba martines

Josephine Zamora nasio el dia
8 de abril en el año de 1948
Sus padrinos son manuel morales
y Trenida morales

arturo Zamora nacio el dia 27 de
Febrero en el año de 1943 sus padrinos
San Tomas fasero y mersedes fusero

U g nasio. Zamora murio
En el año 1977
m_____
merredes. fusero
murio 1988
Eustasio Zavala
murio 1982
anita Zavala
murio 1971

Ledger Book Page showing Birthdates (2)

Our Mother Maria Carmelita (Carmen) Morales/Zamora
passed away February 07, 1952 after 23 years of
marriage. By this time Frances, Cecilia and Eleno lived on

their own in Albuquerque. Candie (Dulcinea), Lala, Christela, and I (Josephine) were home in Manzano.

Dad (Santiago) passed away on November 30, 1996 he was 94 years old. He was admitted to St. Joseph's Hospital hospitalized for a stroke which left him unable to eat or speak. The night of his death he signed to me that he wanted a shave. Eleno, his only son, shaved him. He signed to his neck –Eleno shaved his neck. Everyone left and he passed two hours later.

15 Leaving the Nest

I left home immediately after graduating from Mountainair High School with sixty dollars to my name which was money received as graduation gifts. We were receiving Welfare benefits at the time and my portion of monthly benefit would terminate once I graduated. Fortunately I had several soft landing places in Albuquerque as all my siblings were living there. It felt natural to move in with my single sister Christela, four years my senior, our cousin Christina and Sally, a childhood friend and the sister to my brother in law Delfin. I had been granted a business school scholarship worth one thousand dollars, therefore, that was my first option until I discovered that it only covered a small portion of the expenses. I was not aware that there were education loans and grants available for low income students.

One thing I knew for sure, I could not live on sixty dollars helping out with grocery money and living rent free. In those days I did not have the confidence to ask questions for fear of appearing dumb. I had no clue as to how to navigate Albuquerque on the city buses so I hit Central Avenue on foot. I stopped anywhere I thought might need a receptionist and asked to complete an application. I had taken short hand, accounting, and typing courses but had no work experience. At a small business a man interviewed me and offered me a position, however, I felt very uncomfortable with his line of questioning and did not show on Monday.

Background: I was raised in a single parent home from the age of three by my Father. This man taught us to keep our eyes open and a keen ear. He instructed us not to trust strangers, not to fall in love simply because a young man showed you his teeth. In other words – get to know the person and character. We were not to take candy, gum, or money from men. We were taught to respect our bodies and not allow males to hug, touch or use profanities. To Dad's dying day he prohibited us from wearing shorts or other revealing clothing. It is my opinion that you grow up with a different skill set when brought up by single male parent.

The decision was made – I would not report to my new job instead I walked to the Employment Office and reviewed the job postings. A summer hire position caught my attention. It was working for the U.S. Geological Survey which was located at the time on the campus of The University of New Mexico which meant I could walk to work. I was fortunate in that I was hired and when the summer ended my position was extended with the understanding that I take a Civil Service exam. I was afraid but eager, nervous, and was not aware that a person could check out books at the public library to brush up. I failed the test twice and informed by mail but refused to admit to my supervisor Elsie. Finally, she called Civil Service Office herself and got my failing results verbally nevertheless she kept me on in the Personnel Office. One of my many duties was answering incoming calls. Elsie observed that I spoke with a heavy Spanish accent and mispronounced words. She recommended that I attend a speech class at UNM. The Speech Pathologist fitted us with ear phones and we practiced correct pronunciation with our student partner. Spanish was my first language and I did speak with a heavy accent. The course was immensely useful and left me with great respect for the profession of speech pathology.

I saw Elsie 50 plus years later at my volunteer position with the National Hispanic Cultural Center and she reminisced about her impression of me. She said I had such a good work ethic, was mature for my age, and was willing to learn and found work to keep busy when my tasks were completed. I was surprised and impressed by her comments. Little did she know how inferior I felt in the surroundings of Anglo-Saxons and highly educated professional geologists, hydrologists, and scientists.

During that time, I met my husband Jose Manuel Padilla (J.M.) got engaged, turned in my resignation, married and moved to California in 1968. Here again, I was not aware that I could have continued a career with Civil Service which would have led to a pension.

I am proud of where and how I was raised. Our parents and ancestors were not wealthy yet they taught us survival skills, street smarts, how to work hard, to be creative, organizational skills, to be frugal, faith in God, persistence, service to family and community, joy for life, love, respect, leadership, eating and exercise habits, and entrepreneurship. We develop these skills in addition to the inherited physical attributes with respect to skin tone, eyes, hair, and stature.

Today I lack for nothing and have accomplished more than I could have ever imagined or dreamed of. My husband Jose (J.M.) and I have traveled the United States and to various countries. My 4 nieces Elena, Edwina, Estella, and Viola have accompanied us as have my sisters Candie, Cecilia, and Gigi. My nephews Julian, Andy, Eddie, and his wife Geri went with us to Japan and China one month prior to the Covid 19 outbreak. Our good friends Stan, Catherine, and Ray have also joined us.

Our son Paul and his wife Marianna have 3 young daughters therefore they are unable to get away for an extended period of time but are able to attend functions that take place on long holiday weekends such as weddings, campouts or family re-unions. Paul was able to join his Father for the last one hundred miles on the Camino de Compostela a 500 plus mile walk two years ago. They enjoy golf and have completed several 5K runs in Las Vegas, Nevada as well.

It has been our privilege to have brought up two sons, Joseph who passed at 25 years of age in 1996 and Paul Anthony. Paul is self-employed and is a Contractor and Realtor. He married his mid-school sweetheart Marianna 26 years ago. We are extremely proud of Marianna as she has a very responsible position with New Mexico Governor Michelle Lujan Grisham. They live in Santa Fe, N.M. and have blessed us with three granddaughters Arianna Margarita 11, Raquel Teresa 9, and Esperanza Dulcinea 8. We are able to contribute to a 529 Plan for their education.

We are passionate about education and know that it is the road in order for our people to compete and succeed. We have established an Endowment Fund through the University of New Mexico for the graduates of Rio Grande High School which was where our sons and Marianna attended.

Rio Grande High School is located in the Southwest quadrant of Albuquerque. It is one of the oldest high schools in Albuquerque founded in 1959. It is located at 2300 Arenal Rd. S.W. You access it by crossing the Rio Grande River and the Railroad tracks. There is farming, ranching, and open spaces in that quadrant of the city. Due to its affordability Spanish speaking New Mexicans and immigrants have settled there and many have established businesses such as tire shops, boutiques, meat markets, and restaurants. It is difficult to attract high quality teachers as people are reluctant because of its reputation for being infiltrated with gangs, drugs, and violence. Although there is some truth to this, there is not enough recognition given to students that have attended UNM, Yale, Stanford and other universities. Many more have become entrepreneurs as it is more affordable and faster than attending a four year college. These young individuals have started small businesses in the trades such as plumbing, electrical, building contractors, tile, carpet, beauty shops, etc. This lack of opportunity in an economically disadvantaged community is what lead us to do our small part to provide assistance to some individuals to further their higher education.

My husband Jose and I would like the endowment scholarship to grow to enable more graduates from Rio Grande High School to attend The University of New Mexico. Your gift to the endowment is greatly appreciated and welcomed and can be made by visiting www.unmfund.org/fund/RGHS or mailed to Two Woodward Center, 700 Lomas Blvd NE, Albuquerque, New Mexico 87102

16 Traditional Recipes
Traditional Foods
Recipes

Throughout this book you have heard mention of the many foods prepared in our kitchens. You find these foods recurring in different families mostly because they were born out of the necessity to make do with the ingredients that were readily at hand. Our ancestors were farmers and ranchers and had access to eggs, flour, milk, butter, lard, etc. which served as the simple ingredients for the dessert & bread recipes included below. Families in those days were quite large and women would prepare dishes that would rendir (go a long ways). Although these were the origins of these recipes, they have remained popular through the generations.

Sopaipillas – Deep-Fat Fried Bread

Sopaipillas are a versatile staple and can be served with a meal as you would any other bread, stuffed and hand held as you would a taco, garnished with beans, chile, cheese, lettuce, and tomato to form a complete meal called a Navajo taco, or as a dessert eaten with honey or sprinkled with powdered sugar as one does a beignet from New Orleans.

Yield: 4 dozen medium sopaipillas

Temperature: 420 Degrees

4 Cups sifted flour
1-½ teaspoon baking powder
1 Tablespoon granulated sugar
1 Tablespoon shortening

1 package dry yeast
¼ cup warm water
1-1/4 cups scalded milk (approx.)

1. Combine dry ingredients and cut in shortening.

2. Dissolve yeast in lukewarm water & add to scalded milk - Cooled.

3. Make a well in the center of dry ingredients. Add liquid to the dry ingredients and work into dough.

4. Knead dough well & set aside about 10 minutes.

5. Roll dough to ¼ inch thickness. Cut in squares and fry in melted shortening at 420 degrees F. (Fry only a few allowing fat to stay hot). The sopaipillas will puff up and become hollow. Cook to light golden.

6. Drain sopaipillas on absorbent towels & serve as described above.

New Mexico Staple Bread
Margaret Padilla

My Mother-in-law Mama (1913 – 1978) made this bread often and in large amounts. When I first came into the family in 1969, I requested her recipe only to find that she, in fact, did not have one. She had been taught to bake bread by her mother. Because I wanted it so badly, she took measures to develop the following recipe which I have been successful with for fifty years. The same recipe is used for loaves or buns which resemble empanadas (turn overs).

Dough preparation:
Dissolve   -1 package yeast into 2 Cups warm water
             – set aside

Sift -   5 Cups white flour
             (I use ½ wheat & ½ white flour)

Add -   1 Tablespoon salt
             2 Tablespoons sugar
             2 Tablespoons shortening

Thoroughly combine above ingredients. Slowly add prepared liquid and knead until all ingredients are absorbed.

Note: Whichever method you choose place dough into large greased bowl and make an indentation forming a cross on the dough. This is asking God to bless your bread. Spread thin layer of shortening on dough, cover, and set to rise for I hour in a warm area of your home. It will double in size.

After 1 hour, return dough to board and knead again prior to rising loaves or buns for I additional hour.

Bun method: First form large egg size balls with the dough. Next spread a small amount of shortening on a cutting board and place ball of dough in the center of the greased area. Apply shortening to your finger tips and spread the dough to form a circle about 5-6 inches in diameter. With a paring knife score dough about ¾ inch away from the center. Fold it over at the scored line. With the paring knife make several dimples on the top of the bun and cut ½ inch slits about 2 inches apart at the side of each bun. Place buns on a baking sheet, cover, allow to rise. Bake at 375 F. about 30 minutes to light gold. These buns can be opened and stuffed therefore becoming a perfect sandwich bread with only one opening.

Loaf method: Divide dough in half, form 2 loaves, place into greased loaf pans. With a paring knife score the loaves across the top every inch or so. Place covered loaves in warm area and allow to rise for 1 hour. Bake 30 – 45 minutes at 375 F.

Tortillas de Harina
(Flour Tortillas)

Tortillas can be made thick or thin, however thick ones must be cooked longer. Some Native New Mexicans prefer them thick so that they can separate small pieces and stuff them with food to eat bite size. When thinner we also break off small pieces and use them to spoon our food in place of using a utensil such as a fork or spoon. Try it!! You'll like it!!

Thin and larger tortillas can be stuffed and rolled up to form any type of burrito and hand held. Perfect for lunch or breakfast on the run. In the mid 1900's my oldest sister Frances said she was ridiculed for taking her school lunch rolled up in a tortilla, so she would eat by herself on the back steps of her high school. Today tortillas are fashionable. My, how times have changed.

Yield: 8 – 12 tortillas
Cooking Time: 2-1/2 – 3 minutes
Temperature: 420 – 450 F.

4 cups all- purpose flour
2 teaspoons salt
2 teaspoons baking powder

4 Tablespoons shortening
1-1/2 cups warm water (approx.).

Note: I like to use ½ white & ½ wheat flour or Only wheat flour.

1. Combine dry ingredients thoroughly and cut shortening into the dry ingredients by hand.
2. Add warm water a little at a time and work dough until smooth and manageable.

3. Knead dough several minutes and then allow it to stand about 10 minutes at room temperature.
4. Form dough into balls the size of a small fist. Next roll them out until they are 6 inches in diameter.
5. Place one at a time on hot, greased skillet or on hot greased griddle at 420 degrees (I put shortening on a double folded paper towel and apply to griddle prior to each tortilla). Cook about 2 minutes on one side. Turn over and cook 1 – 2 minutes longer or until done.

Serve as a bread with meals. (When hot off the griddle they are wonderful with butter!)

Natillas or Atole Leche
(Custard Pudding)

Yield: 6 to 8 servings
Cook: 30 to 45 minutes
Temp: Low

The secret to preparing all the recipes I am sharing is "patience." Take time as one would in the preparation of a gourmet meal and pay close attention. Natillas must be cooked on low heat and stirred constantly to prevent the custard from sticking to the bottom of pan. Use a heavy gauge saucepan if possible.

> 1 quart milk
> ¾ cup sugar
> 1/8 teaspoon salt
> 1 teaspoon vanilla
>
> 4 eggs, separated (save whites)
> 1/3 cup flour
> 1-1/2 teaspoon nutmeg or cinnamon

1. Add the sugar, salt and vanilla to the milk and scald in saucepan at 260 F.
2. Make a paste with the egg yolks, flour and one cup of the scalded milk.
3. Add this thickening to the prior scalded milk and continue to cook until it reaches a soft custard consistency. Empty custard into a nice glass serving bowl which has ample space for the beaten egg whites.
4. In a separate medium to large glass bowl beat the egg whites with an electric mixer until they form stiff peaks. Gently fold them into the custard and dust with nutmeg or cinnamon.
5. Spoon custard into individual dishes. (You might add your favorite wafer).

Note: Natillas are best served at room temperature. To hold for a while I recommend you place the bowl in a larger bowl with ice rather than placing them in the refrigerator.

Bizcochitos
(Anise flavored sugar cookies)

Yield: 5 dozen –medium size
Temperature: 350 degree F.
Bake time: Approx. 10 minutes

Bizcochitos are the most popular Christmas cookie in New Mexico and can be prepared early in the season as they freeze well. The size and thickness can be adjusted to your preference.

When Paul married Mariana, my husband J.M. and I baked 60 dozen bizcochitos for the reception. We wrapped 6 cookies in tulleing along with Bible verses and other one liners of their choosing (similar to a fortune cookie) then tied a ribbon to match the wedding colors. These were set at each place setting for guests to enjoy.

Preparation:

6 cups sifted flour
3 teaspoon baking powder
1 teaspoon salt

1 pound lard or butter
1-1/2 cups sugar
2 teaspoons anise seed
2 eggs
¼ cup brandy or wine
1/4 teaspoon sugar
1 Tablespoons cinnamon

1. Sift flour with baking powder and salt.
2. Cream shortening with sugar and crushed anise with electric mixer. Add flour mixture periodically and brandy to form a smooth dough.
3. Knead slightly and break into 2 portions. Roll to ¼ inch or 1/2 inch thick and cut in fancy shapes.

4. In a separate bowl combine sugar and cinnamon. (I prepare 1 cup sugar and about 6 - 8 Tablespoons cinnamon).
5. Bake approx. 10 minutes or until lightly browned.

Note: You can dunk the cookie in the cinnamon sugar prior to baking however I like to immerse the bizcochito in the cinnamon sugar the minute it is removed from the oven taking care not to burn your fingers.

Chapter 13 describes the method used for shaping the cookies by our ancestors.

Arroz Duce
Sweet Rice

Prior to her stroke in my sister Cecilia prepared her rice as described below but added her twist at the end. She folded in one container of whipped cream making the dish lighter and a bit fluffy. It was a Big Hit!!

Preparation:

    1 cup long grain white rice
    2 Tablespoons butter
    2 cups water

    2 cups milk
    1 Tablespoon flour
    1/3 cup sugar
    1 egg
    1-1/2 teaspoon vanilla

    1 cup milk
    2/3 cup heavy cream
    ½ cup raisins
    ½ teaspoon cinnamon

Bring the rice, butter, and water to a boil in a large saucepan over high heat. Reduce heat to medium low, cover, and simmer until the rice is tender. (liquid now absorbed) Approx. 20 – 25 minutes.

Whisk 2 cups milk, flour, sugar, egg, and vanilla extract in a separate bowl. Pour the milk mixture over the cooked rice stirring to combine, and simmer over low heat for an additional 15 minutes.

Stir in 1 cup milk, heavy cream, and raisins until thoroughly mixed. Add to hot rice. Dust with cinnamon, allow to cool and serve.

17 Food for Thought

Our culture has many traditions. Cuentos (story telling) was very popular in the old days. I want to leave you with a Cuento which I hope paints a picture of the way I feel about all the places, people, and experiences that I have lived through.

Cuento/Tale

Once upon a time there lived a man who moved from town to town in search of "The Perfect" place to live.
When asked "Why did you leave Bosque?"
He replied "The people there were not friendly".

When asked "Why did you leave Taos?"
He replied 'The weather was too cold and people were not helpful".

When asked "Why did you leave Arroyo?"
He replied "The people were envious and hateful, I just don't know where to settle down"

By contrast:

Once upon a time there lived a man who moved from town to town.
 When asked "Why did you leave Bosque?"
He replied "I hated to leave as it was so beautiful and
The people were so loving, however work took me to Taos"

When asked "Why did you leave Taos?"
He replied, "Taos brought me so many opportunities and I loved everyone there but I left to help my aging parents".

When asked "Why did you leave Arroyo?"

He replied "All the places I have lived have prepared me for Retirement and I could live in any of those places.

I am free to travel now and I know that people are good everywhere.

I will explore new adventures until the Lord calls me home".

Made in the USA
Las Vegas, NV
15 December 2020